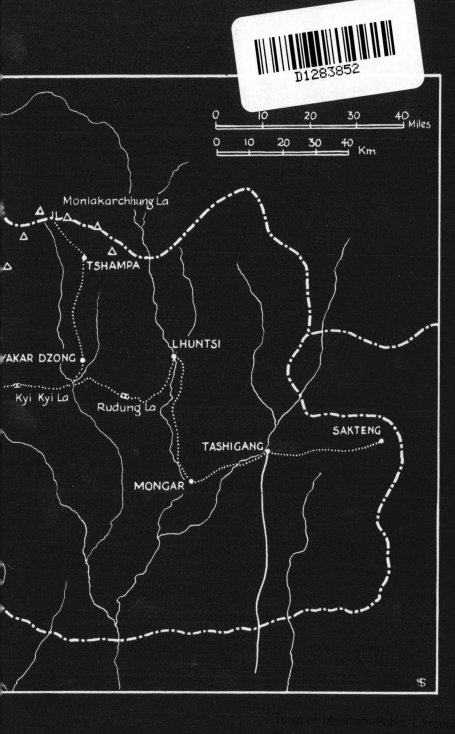

D1283852

Monlakarchhung La

TSHAMPA

Monlakarchhung La

LHUNTSI

AKAR DZONG

Kyi Kyi La

Rudung La

SAKTENG

TASHIGANG

MONGAR

0    10    20    30    40 Miles

0    10    20    30    40 Km

Town of Markham, Public Libraries
Thornhill Community Centre Branch
7755 Bayview Avenue
Thornhill, Ontario L3T 4P1

3 9158 00122193 7

915.15
Ste
IN STACKS

STEELE, Peter                    T2

Two and two halves to Bhutan

WITHDRAWN

Taktsang Gompa

# TWO AND TWO HALVES TO BHUTAN

*A family journey in the Himalayas*

by

PETER STEELE

*Line drawings by*
*Phoebe Bullock*

HODDER AND STOUGHTON

Markham Twp. Public Library
Thornhill Branch

Copyright © 1970 by Peter Steele
Line drawings Copyright © 1970 Hodder and Stoughton

First printed 1970

ISBN 0 340 12923 9

All rights reserved. No part of this publication may be
reproduced or transmitted in any form or by any
means, electronic or mechanical, including photo-
copy, recording, or any information storage and
retrieval system, without permission in writing from
the publisher.

*Printed in Great Britain*
*for Hodder and Stoughton Limited,*
*St. Paul's House, Warwick Lane, London, E.C.4,*
*by Richard Clay (The Chaucer Press), Ltd.,*
*Bungay, Suffolk*

To the wives and children of Himalayan travellers
who have had to stay at home,
and to Sarah, Adam and Judith
who didn't.

# GLOSSARY

N=Nepali    T=Tibetan    B=Bhutanese

| | |
|---|---|
| *ayah* (N) | nursemaid |
| *bhatti* (N) | wayside inn, tea-house |
| *boku* (T) | man's costume |
| *chang* (T) + (B) | home-brewed beer |
| *char* (N) | tea |
| *chuba* (T) | woman's dress |
| *chura* (N) | roasted fried rice |
| *chorten* (T) + (B) | religious shrine |
| *chhu* (T) + (B) | river |
| *dal-bhat* (N) | lentils and rice |
| *dasho* (B) | senior government officer |
| *dekchi* (N) | cooking pot |
| *didi* (N) | woman, sister |
| *dzo* (T) | female yak |
| *dzong* (T) + (B) | fort, regional centre |
| *gaylong* (T) + (B) | young monk |
| *gompa* (T) + (B) | temple, monastery |
| *jangali* (N) | wild-looking |
| *kabngy* (B) | ceremonial scarf |
| *kira* (B) | woman's costume |
| *ko* (B) | man's costume |
| *kukri* (N) | Gurkha knife |
| *lama* (T) + (B) | monk, priest |
| *mane wall* (T) + (B) | prayer wall |
| *mendong* (T) | prayer wall |
| *momo* (T) | dumplings |
| *paise* (N) | money |
| *patouka* (N) | woman's waist scarf |
| *puja* (N) | religious ritual |
| *pukka* (N) | correct |

| | |
|---|---|
| *rakshi* (N) | home-brewed spirits |
| *stupa* (N) | shrine |
| *thanka* (T) + (B) | religious painting |
| *tsampa* (T) | ground roasted barley |
| *yak* (T) + (B) | mountain cattle |

Place names have been transliterated by the Permanent Committee on Geographical Names from field-collected Tibetan script according to the Gould-Richardson system. Points arising from this treatment of the names may be referred to the P.C.G.N. at the Royal Geographical Society, 1 Kensington Gore, London, S.W.7.

---

The manuscript of this book has been corrected and approved for publication by His Majesty the King of Bhutan.

---

I wish to thank Mrs. Irene Fleming and Mr. Patrice Charvet for teaching me the elements of language and correcting the proofs and Dr. Tsewang Pemba for helping me with Tibetan and Bhutanese details.

# ILLUSTRATIONS

# FOREWORD
## *by* ERIC SHIPTON

The invasion and subjugation of Tibet by the Chinese Communist armies was one of the most tragic events of modern times; not only because it resulted in the annihilation and torment of countless innocent victims, but also because mankind is in imminent danger of losing one of its ancient and most successful cultures. For, whatever its imperfections in terms of modern democracy and in spite of its material poverty, the Tibetan theocratic system seems to have produced a people as content, as tolerant, as courageously independent and as free from cramping taboos as can be found anywhere. Today Bhutan is almost the only place where this remarkable culture still thrives on its native soil. Like Tibet itself, this small mountain kingdom has remained beyond the reach of all but a very few Western travellers. Like Tibet, too, it has in the past owed its immunity to foreign influence largely to the policy of the Government of India to defend the political integrity of neighbouring states. Unlike Tibet, it is still independent though how long it will retain this happy position few would dare to guess.

Following upon a spell of medical research in Nepal, Peter Steele was invited by the King of Bhutan to do similar work among his people. Travelling with his family in spartan simplicity, living and working in close contact with all classes of Bhutanese society, Peter took full advantage of his rare privilege for he was thus able to get on intimate terms with villagers and officials alike and to see far more of their way of life than most visitors. He gives us a penetrating and delightfully uninhibited account of this beautiful land and its warm-hearted people.

Peter is also to be congratulated in having a wife who shares his tastes. It is not every woman who would be willing not only to face the hazards and hardship of five months' rugged travel and rough living but to accept the responsibility and anxiety of taking her two small children. People today are apt to forget how readily most children adapt themselves to strange circumstances; and it is not altogether surprising that these two met their adventures with complete nonchalance and enjoyed them as much as their parents – sometimes perhaps a good deal more. In fact they proved a valuable asset in helping to win the confidence and affection of the country people. Though, alas, they were both too young to remember their unique experience, much of it will surely remain to stir their imaginations in later life.

Bhutanese Silver Bowl, Knife and Pan-box

## CHAPTER I

Place names have a quality of magic; but once the places are seen, even if their reputation stands, the magic is never as vivid again. Bhutan has such a ring of enchantment; a tiny kingdom in the Himalayas wedged between Tibet and Sikkim, few people have written about it, a fact that points to its isolation and gives it an aura of mystery.

Our voyage began in London one April morning in 1964. The trees in Hyde Park looked dank in the pouring rain and big red buses ploughed through puddles splashing half-awake office girls hurrying to work. I crossed Park Lane and dashed for shelter into the Dorchester Hotel where I had an appointment with the King of Bhutan.

I was shown upstairs and knocked with trepidation on a large door that was flung open by a member of the Bhutanese Royal Bodyguard wearing national costume, a silver sword tucked into the folds of his tunic. Without a word he led me down a dark corridor into an ante-room where I waited. Anxious to observe the correct etiquette for such an occasion, I had spent much of the previous day searching for a suitable ashi kadar, the white scarf given as a sign of respect and greeting by Tibetans and Bhutanese alike. All I had managed to buy remotely resembling my needs was a two-guinea white silk evening scarf, which I had folded carefully in my pocket in case an occasion for presenting it should arise.

A door was opened by a retainer and His Majesty King Jigme Dorji Wangchuk came in. He immediately put me at ease and my apprehension vanished as we talked quite informally.

"This is the day for seeing my doctors," he said. I was thereby grouped with four doyens of the profession and was deeply, though undeservedly, honoured.

The King was dressed in Bhutanese costume; he wore a gold and red hand-woven boku, a tunic like the Tibetan chuba, hauled above the knees and tied with a belt forming a voluminous pouch; his white cuffs were turned back six inches and he wore long socks and leather shoes. He was a man of powerful build, his face gentle in feature, heavily boned and strikingly handsome. He offered me a cigarette from an engraved silver case. I realised this was no dream – from the window I saw buses roaring towards Hyde Park Corner – reality had returned.

We discussed whether I could come to Bhutan in the future (I had just signed a contract to work in Labrador for a year and so was not free at that time) and he explained some of the problems of medicine in his country.

"You mustn't commit yourself to working in a country like Bhutan before you've seen what it's like," said the King. "When you find you're free, come to Bhutan and bring your wife, as she must like it too."

Once outside I sat down in the bus and put a hand in my pocket for a handkerchief; the silk scarf was still there.

For months my mind reeled at the thought of a visit to Bhutan and my head slowly came out of the clouds. Sarah, my wife, is used to my day-dreaming and in her quiet way left my bout of wild enthusiasm to burn itself out.

One miserable November day in 1966 I returned to our squalid little flat in Cambridge just after the results of the examination for which I had been working during the previous twelve months had come out. I felt we all needed a change after the purgatory of a year's hard study.

14

"Why don't we go to Bhutan?" I asked Sarah, whose equable temperament is a complement to my own impetuosity. She was down-to-earth and practical and as I might have expected my question was coolly received. Her concern was what to do with our two children, Adam aged three and a half and Judith, whom we had adopted as a baby in Newfoundland eighteen months before. I said I had no intention of leaving the children behind and from that moment Sarah joined in the planning.

Permission – this word was much on my mind during the next weeks. My first step was to send a telegram to the King of Bhutan but no one on the overseas exchange could tell me how to do so as Bhutan was not then listed on the international coding. I described Bhutan to the operator in schoolboy geographical language as mid-way between Calcutta and Lhasa, east from Gangtok and west of Assam. Soon the problem was solved and the message went out:

"Doctor Steele available visit Bhutan for six months following your suggestion. Please signify your approval soonest. Deepest respects."

Throughout the preparations I held the belief that the King would surely hold to the word of his invitation three years before and I had an inexplicable faith that somehow we would reach Bhutan.

From the earliest times frontier closure and isolation have characterised the history of Bhutan; the few foreigners who have been able to get permission to enter the country can be counted on one's fingers. Present-day restrictions are not due to insularity or lack of hospitality, but rather to the fact that Bhutan lies within the Indian Inner Line security area, extending along the whole of Northern India within fifty miles of the Tibetan (now Chinese) frontier. The Indian Government has no control over the independent kingdom of Nepal, which forms a breach in their Himalayan border, but it does advise the autonomous kingdoms of Bhutan and Sikkim on their external affairs and defence, although committed not to interfere in their internal administration. It is not possible to enter Bhutan from the south without crossing the Inner Line, for which a permit is required, and the Indians have been unwilling to allow travellers into these buffer areas between China and herself. This political sensitivity has been heightened since the 1962 Chinese invasion of India in the Ladakh region of northern Kashmir and in the North East Frontier Agency (N.E.F.A.) region of Assam, which lies within a few miles of the eastern Bhutanese border.

Permits are given to foreigners only on the request of the Government of Bhutan to the Indian Ministry of External Affairs in Delhi and this virtually means only by personal invitation of the King or a member of the royal family. So I refused to believe my permit would not arrive some day, somehow, even if I had to go and look for it myself – which I did.

I had applied for permission to go to Bhutan; but for what reason could I go? This problem was easily solved. First, I had planned an endemic goitre research project in 1962 to be carried out in the Gilgit region of the Karakoram Himalaya following my work in Nepal. This had fallen through because the Sino-Indian war broke out at the time of our proposed entry, so transferring my plan to Bhutan was not difficult. Second, I had been introduced to Dr. Mourant, the world expert on blood group distributions, who wanted to have specimens from central and eastern Bhutan in connection with his work for the International Biological Programme. Third, there were mountains to climb and new ground to explore.

I met Dr. Mourant in the Serological Population Genetics Laboratory at the back of a tall Victorian office block off Smithfield Market. He helped me to tidy up the details of my endemic goitre survey and to plan a genetics study of blood groups and abnormal haemoglobins, for which I was given a generous grant by the Royal Society.

I was also supported by the Mount Everest Foundation, a fund set up after the climbing of Everest in 1953, with money earned from the film and from lectures, to encourage scientific work in mountain regions. I met Eric Shipton, whom I had known for some years, in the Royal Geographical Society and we searched out all the maps of Bhutan – few existed and the detail of these was thinly spread; in the west and north some mapping had been done but the centre and east of Bhutan was almost blank. His interest encouraged me and I half jokingly asked him if he would like to

16

accompany me. I told him that if I could get permission when I eventually reached Bhutan myself I would cable him. Tentatively we agreed to meet on April 1st at Bumthang in the middle of Bhutan; sadly this never came about but the margin by which we failed was only a hair's breadth. I was given permission for his entry by the King but he failed to receive my cable. Grateful for his help and encouragement I returned from the heights of dreamland to the mundane round of a general practice locum tenens in Cambridge, squeezing all my preparations in between surgeries and visits. Cambridge was in the season of mists that rose from the river, permeating and dampening every corner of life. The era of the mini-skirt was launched and I treated the first mid-thigh chilblain of my career; even in Labrador vanity never rose so high during winter.

During the days of frenzied preparation many people gave me the benefit of their experience. I spent an hour in the library of the Travellers' Club with Sylvain Mangeot, a journalist who had attended the royal wedding and coronation as a friend of the Queen of Bhutan from the days when she was being educated in England. Over china tea and asparagus sandwiches he described the recent history of Bhutan, which sounded like some fantastic historical novel, and he explained the complex events accounting for the country's recent disruptions.

In moments of discouragement when I was ready to abandon the whole scheme Sylvain Mangeot's often repeated words, "Peter, you *must* go," spurred me on. He introduced me to Tsewang Pemba, a fellow trainee surgeon sitting the same exams, who gained the prize for top marks in a field of four hundred competitors – a remarkable achievement for a Tibetan. Three years of his adventurous life had been spent in Bhutan, where he worked as a doctor and married a Bhutanese wife. He gave me a first-hand picture of life in Bhutan and explained some of the problems we would meet.

December was approaching and still no word had come from Bhutan. Adam and I went for walks along the river kicking up cascades of dead leaves; Judith kept Sarah company at home. Our two children were leading a very conventional town life and little did they realise how different their routine would be in three months' time. Sarah did, but she preferred not to think about it and just carried on, stoical and unperturbed.

Two days after I had taken flight to India on my own to seek out the reply to my telegram, a cable arrived inviting me to Bhutan.

Tibetans

## CHAPTER 2

The heat was stifling in the east of Arabia and a haze shimmered on the tarmac where our plane was parked for refuelling. Arabs glided noiselessly about their business casting a sinister air on a situation that seemed strangely clandestine when I paused to consider why I was there. The date was December 9th, the arbitrary day I had chosen to go to India to search for our permits if they had not already arrived. Sarah and I had reluctantly agreed there was no guarantee that the permits would come; we could not wait indefinitely as I would soon be out of work and our flat lease was expiring. I had decided to go to India and to summon Sarah and the family when all plans were smoothly laid for our entry into Bhutan. Meanwhile Sarah would take the children to her home in Suffolk for Christmas.

The chatter of Urdu rose to a pitch as evening fell – the hour of prayer. On board a time-worn jet aeroplane of an Arab airline a motley crowd of Pakistanis and Indians were returning home. A small metal plaque on the engine casing inscribed "Rolls Royce" boosted my sagging confidence. Since the moment I had bought my ticket at half the normal fare from a travel agent in London the journey had assumed the character of an illegal exploit. I had to pay cash to the agent, who excused himself and slipped across the road to collect the tickets from an undisclosed intermediary. Next day after taking leave of Sarah in London I was flown by Swissair to Zurich, where we changed to a Lebanese airline. We rose across the Alps, tinged in the pink twilight afterglow and spectacular in deep shadowed relief.

In Beirut I scribbled a postcard home to reassure my family and drank a cup of black Turkish coffee, the fragrance of which stimulated many memories of our journey through the Middle East in 1962, when shortly after our marriage we had motored to India.

Again we changed planes for our onward journey to Karachi and Bombay, where we landed after a journey of nineteen hours.

Meanwhile at home Sarah was dealing with many problems concerning the medical equipment and drugs we had ordered; she was also packing up our flat in Cambridge and preparing for Christmas in Suffolk. During this time she thanked me neither for my mad schemes, nor for leaving her alone with so much to manage. Sarah's mother eased the burden by handling some of the business matters. The children were not at their easiest in the days after their typhoid innoculations and Sarah assured me she was at a low ebb by the time Christmas arrived.

I was met at Bombay Airport by Sateesh Gupte, a doctor friend; he drove down the middle of the road into Bombay talking and gesticulating wildly as if to catch up on lost time. Impressions of India came flooding back. Bullock carts ambled down the centre of the heavily cambered road, their drivers occasionally aroused from sleep by the raucous honking of cars that swept past heading them towards the ditch. Young girls in rags carrying brass pitchers on their heads moved with a graceful poise that overshadowed the poverty and filth of the hovels they lived in. Lanky men in dhotis with umbrella handles stuck in their shirt collars balanced along the narrow sewerage pipes, which ran across boggy marshland and refuse tips towards the centre of the city. High-gaffed fishing boats, their nets drying, were drawn up on the beach. The "Queen's Necklace", the long curving waterfront of Bombay, was spectacular in its nightly illumination. In the centre of this highway holy cows meandered unmolested, lay on the pavements or chewed at vegetable leaves from the stalls of barrow merchants.

People were everywhere; a pulsating mass of human beings; the seething millions of India. I was reminded of a headline in a Calcutta newspaper at the outbreak of the Sino-Indian conflict in 1962 which read, "One third of the world's peoples are at war with another third."

At Sateesh's home we had a hot curry dinner, eating with our fingers off large metal plates; sweat broke out on my forehead and no water would quench the burning of my tongue – a foretaste of many meals to come. I was tired after the long air journey and lay awake for a while listening to fans whirring, cicadas chirping in the oleander trees and the gentle lapping of waves on the sea shore close by that lulled me to sleep.

Next day I had to move on to Delhi so Sateesh took me to the airport. I was "chance no. 3" on the reserve list but obtained a seat, arriving in the capital two hours later. While waiting for my baggage I watched the apparently purposeless comings and goings of a mass of people; Sikhs in coloured turbans, handsome and arrogant; little Parsees and men in Jinnah caps with high-buttoned jackets; swarthy airforce officers with handlebar moustaches in blue blazers with club badges; well fed ladies in saris, rolls of flesh protruding from under their short-cut blouses; and the ubiquitous depressed looking coolies hanging around in expectation of a few paise.

During the next few days in Delhi I stayed with Suman Dubey, a friend from Cambridge who was on the successful Indian Everest Expedition of 1965. I spent the daytime rushing around government offices; in the cool of evening we sat on wide lawns under pipal trees sipping iced drinks carried by uniformed bearers. Flowers bloomed everywhere, trees were in blossom and the temperature was never more than pleasantly warm. Once again it was difficult to draw myself away from such warm-hearted Indian hospitality but my business lay in Calcutta.

At the station I was involved in a demonstration by a protesting horde of students who were delaying our train. We barricaded ourselves into the compartment and drew all the blinds as a howling mob marauded up and down the platform, smashing glass. A serviceman in my coach had a rifle which he appeared quite ready to use should the need arise. The mob eventually quietened; we left several hours late and travelled across the endless Ganges plain through Agra, Kanpur, Benares and so to Calcutta, where my friend Shamiran Nundy's family were my hosts on and off for the next few weeks.

I visited the Bhutan Trade Commission where all Bhutanese business going through India is transacted. I was expected and received a letter of welcome from Dr. Tobgyel; a large army parade was due to take place in Thimphu that week so he suggested that I should wait until after Christmas before going up to Bhutan.

My Inner Line permit was assured but my main problem was to establish the fact that Sarah and the children were following shortly and that their permits should be hastened. Much confusion and interchange of telegrams took place before the matter was settled. In a moment of elation I wrote to Sarah:

"I am allowing myself to get excited for the first time as I really see us going to Bhutan in the next weeks, whereas up to now it has all been a tenuous myth, an improbable dream. It is just as well we had faith in our hard work, or we might well have given up in the many moments of doubting."

In the next few days I was busy with preparations. I ordered foam rubber mattresses, asked a firm to make insulated boxes for cooling blood specimens, procured some large plastic bags, bought chutney and chocolate and did a hundred little business errands – a familiar story to those setting off for long periods of time into the unknown.

On December 22nd I flew from Calcutta to Bagdogra adjacent to the foothills which rise sharply to the north. I shared a taxi to Darjeeling with a Japanese tourist, an Indian clerk going on holiday and a Gurkha soldier returning home on leave. On the plains around Siliguri are many large tea plantations; uniform rows of short bushes are interspersed with tall eucalyptus trees, which offer shade to the pickers. We soon entered dense forest similar to the jungle strip of Terai below the Mahabarat Hills of Nepal, an area rich in tigers and other big game. The sun set quickly after a brief twilight and we raced on into the darkness.

Our Nepali driver held the wheel in one hand spinning round sharp turns, his other arm hung out of the window and banged ecstatic greetings on the car door every time he passed a friend approaching from the opposite direction. Both cars simultaneously put off their headlights and drove with sidelights alone. An additional hazard was the railway track which followed the course of the road, sometimes crossing it and rising by a series of sharp angled bends and complete loops. We could hear the distant noise of the train hooter and see the engine spotlight above us approaching through the trees. Soon it was upon us; we mounted the bank to get clear of the track and were enveloped in reams of thick smoke, which cleared to show the red tail light of the guard's van disappearing into the jungle below. In the darkness we remained unaware of a precipitous drop from the outer edge of the road that plunged several thousand feet to the valley. At halfway we stopped to let the engine cool and to refresh ourselves with tea served in glasses and laced with sugar that crusted the rim and lay thick on the bottom; sickly sweet pastries and biscuits settled heavily on the stomach. Beside us in the bhatti, or tea-house, Nepali coolies squatted on their haunches resting before the next stage of their journey. These hill people contrasted markedly with the countless masses of Calcutta, so recently left behind. Darjeeling is in the province of West Bengal but its character and population is almost pure Nepali.

Late that night the lights of Darjeeling appeared like a sparkling ribbon stretching along the hillside spur on which the town is built high above the Rangit Valley. Mrs. Pemba welcomed me, Tsewang having asked her to arrange my accommodation. I received the traditional Tibetan cup of hot butter tea with grease floating in globules on the surface, the strong flavour of salt making it taste more like broth than tea. A plateful of momo, minced meat covered with boiled suet, was produced and I exchanged polite greetings with the many Tibetans present. I passed on news of Tsewang to which they listened with rapt attention as if to the epic of a conquering hero. After a congenial meal I was escorted up the hill by several Tibetans wrapped in their long chubas and with high leather boots. The moon shone and a sharpness in the air froze our breath. The atmosphere was crystal clear and beyond the roofs of the houses row on row of hills in sharp relief rolled gently towards the foot of Kangchenjunga, like an army arrayed in ranks before its commander. The great mountain, 28,156 feet in height, flanked by Pandim and Nursing, dominated the panorama and appeared deceptively close in the moonlight.

The following morning I sat in the Chowrasta, an open square which straddles the ridge at the highest part of the town and overlooks tiers of houses piled above the bazaar and market place. In the warm sun I watched many Himalayan tribesmen pass by against a backcloth of mountains; the Kangchenjunga massif lay in the west and the peaks of Sikkim to the north. Barefoot Nepali coolies with bulging neck muscles carried heavy loads in wide bamboo baskets supported by a head-band. They wore black sidecaps and patoukas wound round their waists into which were stuffed their worldly treasures and a handsome kukri knife. Carrying equally heavy loads a few paces behind walked their didis, the women, wearing purple velvet blouses and colourful saris. All their wealth was turned into jewellery; they wore gold earrings, necklaces and bangles, and diamond studs through their noses. These people were mostly Lepchas, Rais and Limbus from Eastern Nepal and Sikkim. Smart Newari and Bengali merchants were taking down the shutters of small shops selling curios to satisfy the appetites of globe-trotting tourists for whom Darjeeling is a popular port of call. Syce boys in charge of the ponies were trying to entice children on to their mounts for a rupee ride round the upper circuit path.

Some elderly Tibetan men and women were perambulating the Chowrasta muttering prayers, the pitch rising and falling like a chant, spinning prayer wheels and telling beads as they walked. They were still dressed in heavy wool-lined coats belted at the waist, with long sleeves wound round the middle or flung loosely over one shoulder. Some Sherpas, noticeable for their smart clothing, a legacy of recent expeditions, marched round with the swagger of Swiss guides.

My peace was shattered by screams of "Hello, uncle" and I was molested by four Pemba children I had seen peacefully asleep the previous night, docile no longer. They had jet black hair, narrow eyes and bright red cheeks like all Tibetans. We made our way to the Buddhist shrine on the hill above the Chowrasta where the family performed their religious rites, the puja, in front of the lama's enclosure. Butter and flour were laid on an altar over which home-brewed beer, or chang, was poured; some pine needles were then thrown into a small oven making a fragrant smoke. The lamas proceeded with their devotions quite unconcerned with four exuberant children clanging bells and spinning prayer wheels. Red robed priests with saffron shirts walked round the shrine murmuring the sacred Buddhist text, "Om mani peme hum." Kangchenjunga could be clearly seen through a forest of prayer flags flapping in the breeze from high poles, carrying their worship towards the distant mountains; only from Pokhara, lying at the foot of Annapurna, have I seen mountains appear so close. Looking down into the deep intervening valleys I remembered the toil of cresting similar ridges and always underestimating the distances. The Tibetan name Kang-chen-dzo-nga means "The great snow mountain with the five treasures" (the five separate peaks).

Beside a leafy bamboo grove a short way off some Tibetan ladies wearing long chubas with richly coloured aprons were having a picnic, a favourite Tibetan pastime. In their Lhasa days they would have ridden a little way out of town to the parks where willow trees lined the streams, and there they would have erected large gaily decorated tents. With food and chang in abundance the party would have danced its way through several days and nights until, finally exhausted, they returned to their homes within the city walls under the dominating Potala Palace.

As I looked far below on the side of the hill where the houses and huts of their refugee encampment stood, I felt a deep sympathy for the Tibetan people. There lived a community of Tibetan families, who had gravitated to this and other centres along the Himalayan border when their country was invaded by the Chinese in 1950. Under the guise of enforcing their suzerainty over the Tibetans by the treaty of 1913, the Chinese armies entered the country and took over the government, installing a puppet in the place of the Dalai Lama, who fled to India. During the honeymoon period of the next six years there was a reasonably peaceful co-existence between the invaders and the indigenous population. After the flight of the Dalai Lama in 1959, monasteries were sacked, lamas murdered and children transported to China for indoctrination. A steady trickle of Tibetans, discontented with the Chinese domination, left the country but after the 1959 purge a mass exodus got under way and many thousands of Tibetans fled south to Nepal and India.

During our work in Kathmandu in 1962, Sarah and I had many dealings with Tibetan refugees as patients and friends, for their camp stood close to the hospital. Then under the care of the International Red Cross, their conditions were pitiable. They lived in bamboo huts, rarely dry during monsoon rains; many of the older ones suffered from tuberculosis and the babies from malnutrition. The stories of recent arrivals to the camp from Tibet were full of horror amounting to insidious genocide. We made several friends to whose houses we went in the evenings, where we were introduced to the courtesy and humour of these people. West of Dhaulagiri we met many nomadic Tibetans wandering and attempting to trade; others were scratching a living from smallholdings. All were without roots, refugees deprived of their homeland and their way of life.

The popular picture of Tibet as some idyllic Shangri-La is false. Life was feudal and harsh for the peasants and a mighty gulf existed between them and the rich. Yet their natural disposition is one of cheerfulness and pride, and keeping these qualities in evidence when they have been deprived of so much is hard. I spent much of that day at the Tibetan centre where a self-help scheme is in operation. All their skills are pooled, be it carpet making or needlework, dairy husbandry or carpentry, so that the Tibetans in the community are no longer dependent on the financial aid of the government or of outside supervision.

At sundown the school children put on a play in their dormitory. Three tiers of bunks were crammed with excited faces of all ages and every inch of floor space was occupied. A make-shift stage had been erected and curtains hung from the rafters. The play was a three hour long epic depicting Lhasa before the invasion, the sub-

26

sequent misfortunes of the people at the hands of the Chinese and their escape from Tibet and flight into India. I found difficulty in following the details but the expressions of rapture, horror, delight and joy that passed over the rows of faces acted as an emotional barometer to the happenings in the play. The audience were appreciative and attentive, creating a tangible atmosphere of unity among these people reliving a tragic recent chapter of their history that will be the mainstay of the folklore of Tibetans in exile for generations to come. Few of those children had ever been in Tibet yet the events were as fresh as if they happened yesterday. The performance took place under a huge photo of the Dalai Lama, their God–King, whose powerful personality has been a force welding together this scattered remnant of the Tibetan people and keeping their culture and religion intact.

On Christmas Eve a loudspeaker in the bazaar broadcast carols over the town; I felt downhearted at being separated from the family at this time and sent a telegram to Sarah asking her to come out on the first possible flight after January 1st. There were times at home with the children howling and work pressing, when I dreamed of nothing better than to be transported on my own into the heart of the Himalayas where I could be at peace. Now that the situation was real I missed them and Sarah greatly. To fill the intervening time I decided to walk north towards Kangchenjunga along the Singalila ridge which divides Nepal from Sikkim and Bengal.

Kangchenjunga coolies

## CHAPTER 3

I took a car to Ghoom, a village that lies about five miles south-west of Darjeeling and looks across jungle foothills to the plains stretching endlessly southwards. To the north lie the mountains.

The old car pinked hard going uphill alongside a heavily laden train. We turned off the main road and began a freewheel descent of several thousand feet through the heart of the tea-gardens built on steep terraced slopes. The tea bushes are smaller than those of the plains standing two to three feet high, and the altitude, the soil and the climate give Darjeeling tea a special flavour. The labour force are mostly Nepali men and women who stand beside the bushes plucking the young shoots and collecting them into sacks.

I waited for two hours in a tea bhatti in Sukia thinking I could get a lift to Manebanjang at the foot of the hill which rises to Singalila. I began to talk with the men sitting in the bhatti drink-ing hot sweet tea who were full of curiosity and friendship when I spoke to them in Nepali. I had taken lessons while in Kathmandu and learnt to write the script so that my pronunciation at first was correctly phonetic, even pukka. During our three months journey in the mountains of West Nepal in company with Tamang coolies I picked up the vernacular – kitchen Nepali as some call it – that was essential to interpret the bawdy songs they sang round the campfire at night, which we could safely sing in front of the missionaries as the dialect was so broad.

One old man of about seventy had served in a Gurkha regiment during the war. His campaigns took him through North Africa ("Montgomery ekdum first-class general") to the landings in Italy; he fought hand-to-hand with his kukri at Monte Cassino, developed a taste for chianti and Italian girls and somehow finished the war in Czechoslovakia. He was now returning from Bhutan after visiting the King, on what pretext I was unable to discover. He displayed the chameleon-like quality of the Gurkhas, who appear at ease whether squatting over a bowl of rice on the mud floors of their thatched houses far away in the hills, riding in red double decker buses in Hong Kong, or immaculate in attendance on Her Majesty the Queen at Buckingham Palace. After their varied experiences soldiering abroad, more remarkable still is the ease with which they return to the hills, where they appear quite contented and without signs of frustration at the lack of benefits, so-called, that the outside world can bestow.

Transport was obviously not available and as it was misty, cold and damp I set off with my overloaded rucksack for Manebanjang five miles away. The dirt road wound through dense forest from which came the cries of many birds and where agile grey monkeys performed gymnastics in the trees. I walked quickly though my legs were out of training and caught up with a boy who showed me short cuts through the trees.

More than an hour later I reached the village in gathering darkness. All my movements were restricted, this being an Inner Line area, so I checked at the police post and showed the pass that had been issued to me at Darjeeling. Cloud descended making the darkness more intense; I knew I would have difficulty in finding the way so I asked if a porter would come with me to Tonglu, the next village at the foot of the big climb on to the ridge. Having thus made my wishes known to the policeman and a crowd of young boys, I sat down and waited. Within ten minutes, in the extraordinary fashion of the East where word is passed round on a lightning bush-telegraph, a strong looking boy appeared. After a few cursory exchanges of figures had settled his wage he picked up my rucksack without visible effort and set off down the road at a trot without so much as a backward glance to see if I was following. He maintained the same pace uphill, down-hill or on the level; with considerable exertion I drew close enough to carry on a conversation. I discovered his name was Robilal, a Tamang by caste. He looked "jangali", meaning a man who has come out of the woods. He had a wild, hunted look in his eyes and black hair with long sideburns; his clothes were ragged and a large kukri was thrust into his patouka; his bare feet were cracked and tanned like boot leather. I was pleased with his companion-ship, which grew quickly and depended little on the spoken word.

We walked at first in swirling mist but soon the moon came out and the scene was beautiful. The road wound along a hillside bordered by rhododendrons and tall ghostly teaks on which grew moss, creepers and orchids. The mist hung in pockets among the trees whose silhouettes were indistinct in the moonlight. We frequently left the steep path to cut short a bend, so reducing the distance a great deal but making energetic climbing. A profound peace reigned; not a sound could be heard except the wind in the trees; on the road ahead we cast soft shadows, which moved with us like silent companions.

Suddenly we left the trees and came upon an open place on the ridge looking down into the Rangit Valley full of cloud lapping up to the bases of the enclosing hills from which dark spurs projected. The clouds above us still drifted across the face of the moon, which gave a silvery sheen to Kangchenjunga standing alone in the distance. This memorable sight was ours for only a few brief minutes, then we were again enveloped in mist, which clung in droplets to our woollen sweaters and formed hoar-frost as we climbed higher into the cold air. Robilal's pace never flagged and after two hours we came to some houses that I thought were the half-way mark to Tonglu. I was overjoyed to find we were only a mile or two away and decided to stay at this village, called Mekma.

A small group of houses and a monastery were situated astride the ridge; a large white chorten, a religious shrine, stood at the entrance to the village flanked by three tall prayer flags. The chorten was the shape of an inverted onion with a square tiered base. Robilal entered the largest house, belonging to the headman of the village, dumped my rucksack on the floor and made himself at home. I followed and we sat round charcoal baskets brought in by the women to warm us, and drank hot, sweet tea, stewed thoroughly. By the activity around the fireplace I guessed that Robilal had ordered food and soon we were squatting on the floor using our fingers to eat a huge platter of dal-bhat – boiled rice and lentils – with fried egg and some green vegetables. The headman sat in a niche beside the fire watching us and questioning Robilal about me. His sinister appearance, which at first I took to be the leonine disfigurement of leprosy, was due to a gun back-firing into his face some years before; he was fortunate not to have injured his eyes as his cheek was extensively scarred. He became garrulous as we drank potent, home-brewed rakshi and enter-tained us with stories of his hunting exploits. I was shown to the family shrine to sleep, while Robilal curled up near the dying embers of the fire.

In the morning heavy frost lay on the grass outside; ice on the roofs of the houses melted as the sun came up, making steam and looking as if the whole village were on fire. We paid our host modestly for his hospitality and set off along the ridge towards Tonglu.

At a crossroads the main track led westwards as the highway to Ilam and East Nepal. For the first hour we enjoyed fine views of the mountains but these were soon obscured by cloud rising out of the valleys. The road climbed and fell gently during the first half of the day; we stopped at a tea bhatti in Kalopokhari where I examined an old woman with a cancer of the stomach for whom, at this late stage, little could be done. We moved on to Gairibas where we lunched and rested before the start of the steep and long climb to Sandak Foo.

I began to feel the immense freedom that comes from wandering in the hills. I was able to detach my mind from the mechanical movements of walking and let it roam widely, to plan, to think of past adventures, or not to think at all and merely to enjoy the beauty of my surroundings. My sense of relaxation was complete; for the first time in a year I had no exams to worry about and was at peace with myself. My only present concern was to reunite the family and myself, to move into Bhutan as soon as possible and to start on my work.

Robilal was a pleasant companion and few words sufficed to establish our needs: "that silence which is the fellowship of the hills" as Geoffrey Winthrop Young wrote. Some people feel happy as lone wolves but I prefer to travel in company with someone to whom I can express my feelings of pleasure and share in talk or silence the joys and miseries of the experience. Robilal's company apart, he proved an asset in carrying my sack, so making the breaking-in period of getting fit more gentle.

From Gairibas we climbed steeply for four hours and broke out on to a meadow just under 12,000 feet, at Sandak Foo. My unacclimatised breathing was becoming laboured towards the end and a leaden feeling pervaded my legs. Being mid-winter it was extremely cold, so we barricaded ourselves in a small hut to keep out the wind, built a roaring fire and soon the room acquired a comfortable warmth. Robilal cooked rice and dal in quantity and we did full justice to the meal. We drew our mattresses round the fire, collected a pile of firewood close to hand so that we could stoke it without leaving our sleeping bags during the night and I wrote my diary by the flickering light of the burning logs.

At 4 a.m. the next morning I rose to watch the sun come up on the mountains. Thick frost lay on the ground and the water butt was frozen solid. In the east a faint pink glow turned a deeper and richer red as the full moon dropped towards its horizon. Suddenly the world was awake and the fireball sun began its steady climb into the sky. Shadows fell in deep folds on Kangchenjunga standing above hundreds of subsidiary peaks; Chomolhari lay to the east and the Natu La to the north; Sikkim was under a blanket of cloud. Westwards the whole Everest massif became lit up; Lhotse, Makalu and Ama Dablam seemed a stone's throw away because of the clarity of the atmosphere, though the distance must have been more than one hundred miles. A snow plume formed by ferocious winds that carry away the fine powdered snow trailed from the summit ridge of Everest – Chomolungma in Tibetan.

A gnarled Himalayan pine in my foreground was a gaunt reminder of the earthliness of the scene.

Too soon these colours were gone and the whole world was suffused with daylight; for a few brief moments I had lived in a place of heavenly beauty.

Our route now followed the Singalila ridge northwards gently rising and falling between 11–12,000 feet. Freezing low cloud of the previous night settled as hoar-frost on the blades of grass forming razor sharp fronds to windwards like miniature prayer flags. We walked partly in woodland, partly in open meadow. When we were in shadow Robilal found the ground cold under his bare feet, the only time of our journey together he expressed feelings of discomfort. Otherwise he kept marching like an automaton and I followed behind.

The skeletons of charred Himalayan pines stood against the sky, their branches pointing horizontally in all directions showing the ravages of a recent forest fire. Three miles short of Phalut we decided to follow the spur into the Rangit Valley, for the clouds were coming up already and we had evidently enjoyed the best views of the day. We met coolies passing in both directions as this was another important trade route between Darjeeling and East Nepal. Some young girls in bright saris were carrying heavy loads in split bamboo cane baskets. Childhood had passed them by and they were plunged prematurely into adult life, missing the carefree time of youth. Two babies were crossing the mountain fast asleep in a basket on their father's back. By the time we reached Siri Khola we had dropped nearly six thousand feet in three hours and being so unfit my knees were aching fiercely. We crossed a small bridge and walked along a wide path following the contours of the valley and maintaining our height. I was tired when we reached Rimbik Bazaar having walked for nine hours with only brief halts for tea.

We stayed in the hotel, or bhatti, in the centre of the bazaar. In the villages on trade routes one or two houses make their living by catering for itinerant travellers; rice and dal is provided at a modest price, with some potatoes and a little chicken curry if one is lucky. Coolies joyfully eat bright red pepper pods for flavouring but the smallest sliver in a curry, mistaken for a piece of tomato skin, made me break out in a profuse sweat and feel as if red hot coals were on my tongue. Tea is always brewing on the embers in a large aluminium pot. Beside the bhatti is a special wall on which the coolies can rest their baskets to unload them from their backs. It is not unusual to find coolies carrying weights of 150–200 pounds and I passed one with five four-gallon jerry cans full of petrol, some kitchen utensils and a load of umbrellas on the top that he had carried for several days.

At the end of a day they relax in the bhatti with their friends, plucking aberrant chin hairs with tweezers or gambling passionately with dice over a drink of rakshi. When night comes and the boasting and singing has subsided, they roll out bamboo mats on the earthen floor and sleep round the fire. I never felt lonely on such journeys and enjoyed being able to share a part of the coolies' lives through my relationship with Robilal. Judging by the remarks he made to fellow coolies, I had obviously risen in his esteem since he discovered I could keep up with the pace he set. Even so, he was like a thoroughbred race horse giving away several stones to me.

We walked through rice country where terraced fields were carved in elegant patterns far up the hillsides, representing generations of labour in their construction and maintenance. Now they were full of short stubble but soon they would be ploughed and prepared for planting before the onset of the monsoon in May. The houses were low and thatched with straw and under the eaves maize pods were hanging for storage. Bananas and other fruits grew abundantly and the red star-shaped lalpatti flower added a splash of colour.

Several hours later at Bijanbari our walk ended and I paid off Robilal. In this feudal society of widely gaping class divisions it is impossible to forget the sahib-servant relationship. I like to think that for a brief spell Robilal and I enjoyed each other's company as fellow men. As soon as he counted his money he crossed the road to a stall and bought a smart blue shoulder bag; I doubted if there would be much left by the time he reached home after a few rounds of drinks and games of dice. I took a jeep ride back to Darjeeling that evening and returned to Calcutta to meet my family.

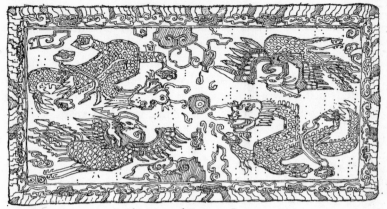

Phoenix and Dragon Carpet

## CHAPTER 4

A big jet plane circled over the runway and came in to land over the tops of the palm tree jungle at the edge of which Calcutta airport is built. Soon I could see the excited faces of Adam and Judith at the window of the bus. Sarah passed through the customs with no trouble, clutching the two children while people on either side had their luggage ransacked. Arriving straight from the middle of an English winter and tired after a long flight, they all looked pale and drawn; Adam's hair was shorn and Judith had a close crop to reduce the trouble from nits.

We took a taxi to an hotel off Chowringhee where Sarah and I had stayed before, and settled in to a comfortable and airy room. Adam took one look at the lavatory and, raising his nose in the air in a derogatory manner, said,

"Charming – and where's the seat?"

Owing to a series of remarkable coincidences our fortunes changed rapidly. I rang a firm of tea brokers to enquire after Richard Warren, a friend of mine, whom I knew was working in Cochin in South India. To my surprise I discovered he had arrived in Calcutta on business the previous day. He talked about us and our proposed journey to one of his colleagues, Colin Burn, whose house was empty as his family were back at school in England. He sent a car to collect us at once.

We found ourselves transported to a spacious and comfortable house in Ballygunge, a desirable suburb of Calcutta, where a household of willing Muslim servants looked after us in a style to which we were quite unaccustomed. Abdul, the major domo, was over six feet tall and wore a fez; at the touch of his master's bell he would leap up the stairs three or four at a time with the agility of a springing tiger that belied his years.

Colin Burn breakfasted in his bedroom, left for the office and re-appeared for dinner in the evening, leaving us the run of his house. The children rarely saw him and Adam talked of the house as "Abdul's Hotel". Sarah and the children settled down to the change of environment and put on some lost weight; I was able to do the final shopping and make arrangements for the transport of my blood specimens back to England.

One afternoon we visited the younger Bhutanese Queen Mother, Ashi Pema Dechen, at the royal family's flat; her daughter, Princess Ashi Choki, who lives in Bumthang in Central Bhutan, was with her. Ashi Pema was gracious and charming; we sat on the edges of our seats making conversation partly in Nepali, partly in English. We were anxious about the behaviour of the children, who sensed the tension and reacted accordingly. Adam started doing monkey tricks and knocked his head on the edge of an ornately carved table; he let out a shriek that reverberated through the building and brought servants running from every direction. Judith howled in sympathy. The cacophony so embarrassed me that beads of perspiration broke out on my forehead; Sarah gathered the children and rode out the crisis with calm. Our hostess was completely unconcerned but we speedily took our leave vowing we would do no more royal visiting until we had someone to take the children "behind the green baize door" in times of stress. This experience brought me up with a jolt, making me realise I must spend time to play with the children and read to them, as I had not been able to do in recent months owing to the pressure of exams. There would be plenty of opportunity in the weeks ahead.

Of the nightmarish afternoon spent clearing our freight in the Calcutta customs I will say little, as the subject occupies a full chapter in many of the accounts written of Himalayan expeditions. I emerged feeling as if I had been squashed by a mountainous load of red tape, brainwashed by the machinations of a topsy-turvy bureaucracy and wrung dry of more rupees than I could spare.

We ate a final breakfast with Colin Burn under the pipal trees on the spacious lawns of the Tollygunge Club, an island of imperial civilisation in the heart of impoverished refugee shanties. I could sympathise with the resident British who cling to the few institutions such as this where they can withdraw from the hostility and poverty around them in order to retain their equanimity. Although one cannot close one's eyes to the presence of insoluble problems, to become emotionally involved in them is frustrating because the poverty is often perpetuated by political inefficiency and corruption over which no amount of goodwill can prevail.

We were now waiting for the arrival of Sarah's Inner Line permit; the Bhutan Trade Office in Calcutta had made formal applications but there was no guarantee how long this permit would take to come. So we decided to move up to the hills, first to Darjeeling and then to Kalimpong, as a better place to step off into Bhutan.

We flew to Bagdogra in a plane Adam disdainfully considered more like the bush aircraft we had used in Labrador than the giant Boeing of his recent flight from England. On reaching Darjeeling we stayed at the Planters' Club situated in the centre of the town and built with generous Victorian proportions. From the balcony we looked down at the pedestrian traffic of the main street and had expansive views over the town to the snows beyond. Coal fires in the bedrooms, good meals and plenty of space for the children to play gave much comfort. We filled the days with pony rides around the Chowrasta circuit and were pleased to see that Adam and Judith settled into the saddle with ease.

We went out to the Himalayan Mountaineering Institute where Tenzing Norkay Sherpa was the chief instructor. He generously invited Sarah and me to attend a lunch party he was giving next day for Sir Edmund Hillary, who was passing through Darjeeling with his family after spending several months in Solo Khumbu setting up a Sherpa hospital. We met at the Gymkhana Club next day for a pleasantly informal meal. Tenzing has been called "the gentleman from Chomolungma" with good reason; he looks an aristocrat despite his humble start as a milk porter in Darjeeling, since when he has become the greatest of Himalayan Sherpa mountaineers. With his natural charm and broad smile, Tenzing acted the part of host as if he had given dinner parties all his life; he took his place at the bottom of the table, surrounded by the New Zealanders' children and his own, joking with them throughout the meal. The occasion gave me opportunity to discuss with the New Zealand doctors, Max Pearl and Michael Gill, their goitre work in Solo Khumbu that had many features in common with my own project. They gave me helpful advice on problems they thought would likely come my way.

Sarah was sitting next to Pem Pem, Tenzing's eldest daughter.

"I know it's very short notice, but do you know of a Sherpa girl who would come to Bhutan with us to help look after the children?"

"How long would you want her for?" Pem Pem asked.

"About six months. We'll be travelling a lot of the time, and I've no idea what she should expect. Unfortunately, we leave for Kalimpong tomorrow."

"I'll see what I can do. My husband will come to the Planters' Club at 8 a.m. tomorrow to tell you if I've found anyone."

We were grateful that Pem Pem should take the trouble; she was the ideal person to look for an ayah, knowing all the Sherpas in Toon Soong Basti, their special colony in the town.

After the meal photographs were taken of Hillary and Tenzing linking arms together fifteen years after their great day on Everest, looking much the same as they did then, unsophisticated, down-to-earth men of the mountains.

At 8 a.m. the following morning a call came from the hall porter to say that Pem Pem's husband, Tschering, was waiting. Beside him stood a short girl dressed in a smart chuba and coloured apron.

"This is Lakpa Doma," he began, "she will come to Bhutan as your ayah. You pay her the standard wage of eighty rupees a

38

month and buy her food and clothing. She will work well for you; Pem Pem has talked with her."

"When can she start?" Sarah asked, not knowing which person to address.

"She must arrange to leave her baby with her parents-in-law, as her husband is away in the army. She will be ready tomorrow."

"Don't hurry, please," Sarah said, "I will give you money for her taxi fare to Kalimpong. Ask her to join us there in three days."

So we acquired our ayah, a girl of eighteen to twenty years, who at a moment's notice was prepared to drop everything to go on a venture lasting for several months, without an inkling of what it would involve.

The following day we went down to the motor stand and took our place in a jeep bound for Kalimpong thirty miles away in a different valley. Our road forked left at Ghoom and began a long descent through a forest of eucalyptus and pine above terraced tea-gardens. We crossed a narrow ridge separating Darjeeling from Kalimpong; hundreds of feet below lay the Teesta River flowing south from Sikkim. After the crisp clear air of Darjeeling it felt hot and sultry in the enclosed valley floor, which was almost at the altitude of the plains. Soon we were climbing again up the eastern hillside through fertile fields and colourful flowering gardens to reach Kalimpong, which lies at 4,000 feet, much lower than Darjeeling and pleasantly warmer in the winter season. This small bazaar was important as the staging post before Gangtok for travellers entering Tibet by the Natu La and the Chumbi Valley going to Gyantse and on to Lhasa. As a hill station Kalimpong was a haven for generations of Europeans from the torrid heat of the Indian summer. Kalimpong Bazaar sits astride a saddle on a steep-sided ridge; to the west the ground falls to the Teesta and looks along the length of the Rangit Khola, spur after spur descending to the valley floor in dogtooth pattern. In the far distance, covered by a light fall of snow, lay Sandak Foo; Darjeeling was just out of sight. Only the summit peaks of Kangchenjunga showed above the intervening hills, which were of rich ochre and burnished pastel shades. Eastwards the mountains of Sikkim on the Tibetan border formed a long chain across the panorama. On the other side of the bazaar gentle hills rolled towards Bhutan, more accessible than the big mountains and having a pastoral atmosphere with small farms scattered on their slopes.

We arrived at the Himalayan Hotel and were greeted by an elderly lady in shirt and slacks, a cigarette in the corner of her mouth,

"Sorry, we're full up."

"But I believe we were booked in yesterday," I said, almost pleading, my disappointment was so profound. "I'd be most grateful if you could find room for us."

"Oh, you must be Dr. Steele. Yes, we were expecting you. Welcome. I'm Annie Perry." Her offhand manner changed to genuine warmth. "Come over here and meet Vera, she looks after the housekeeping. Vicky hasn't got up yet, she only does the gardening these days."

We walked across to the lawn to where a patterned Tibetan awning shaded some chairs; a blaze of colour filled the flower beds and the morning mist was rising from the valleys. Seated under the canopy, wearing a wide brimmed hat and a voluminous Tibetan chuba, was a portly, smiling lady with a sun-tanned complexion.

"You must make yourself at home," she said, "and the children can go where they like. Is there anything they don't like to eat? I hear you're going into Bhutan."

"Yes, but there's been some delay over Sarah's permit," I explained, "so the family may be here some time. I expect to go in a few days' time."

"She can stay as long as she likes. The hotel will be empty when the New Zealand party leave."

To meet such kindness was a great comfort and made the prospect of leaving the family to wait for their permit much easier. My permit to enter Bhutan was due to expire shortly; I therefore had to reach Bhutanese soil so that it could be extended rather than my having to make a new application.

The hotel used to be the family home of David Macdonald, a former British trade agent in Yatung, the first town one reaches on entering the Chumbi Valley of Tibet from Sikkim. Three of his daughters, Mrs. Annie Perry, Mrs. Vicky Williams and Miss Vera Macdonald are the formidable ladies who now run the hotel. Beautiful Tibetan rugs covered the floors and seats, priceless thankas hung on the walls and a collection of Tibetan metal work teapots and bowls stood in the hall. The sisters have maintained a family atmosphere of relaxation and informality.

We drew up chairs beside Auntie Vera, who told us the story of her family. David Macdonald's father was a Scot and his mother a Sikkimese lady of noble birth; he married a half Nepali wife and had thirteen children, nine of whom survived. In 1904 he accompanied the Younghusband Expedition to Lhasa and remained as British trade agent in Yatung, where his wife, Alice, ran the school. Annie, the eldest daughter, when only fourteen years old, used to bring four of the children on the twelve day journey to school in Darjeeling. During storms on the Natu La the children would bury their heads in the wide sleeves of the Tibetan horsemen for shelter. When their mother was ill, Annie covered the distance home in a record three days and three nights, with change horses ready prepared at each stage. In 1925 the family left Tibet after twenty years and David Macdonald retired to Kalimpong.

We settled quickly into the hotel. Adam made friends with Jigme, the son of the junior bearer, and they spent happy hours building aeroplanes and rockets with a wooden construction kit we brought from home, or hanging like monkeys from the branches of trees. Judith was still bewildered by her change of environment.

The following day Lakpa Doma arrived from Darjeeling to start work as our ayah. The children were suspicious at first and Judith howled, but Lakpa soon made friends and from that moment on took Judith completely under her wing. Sarah took them down to the bazaar and all three were measured for new Tibetan chubas. Indians look askance at a mini-skirt and I am sure one has never been seen in Bhutan; the chuba proved much easier for sitting on the floor and on low benches with decorum.

Judith and Lakpa began to make expeditions each afternoon, a habit they kept up for the next four months. We could never discover where they went or what they did but however they passed the time their outings were evidently a great success. Auntie Vera took Sarah aside and instructed her on the management of servants.

"On no account must you spoil your ayah or she'll become lazy. Be strict but fair."

We could follow her instructions in Kalimpong when other servants were around, but Lakpa soon became a part of the family when we moved to Bhutan.

I made a brief visit to Gangtok, the capital of Sikkim, on a special permit, granted much to my surprise as it has been strictly military territory since the 1962 fighting. Large concentrations of Indian troops were stationed in Sikkim, determined not to be caught unprepared again by the Chinese.

In the company of a Tibetan businessman, a Sikkimese soldier, a Nepali coolie and a dhoti-clad Bengali, I travelled by jeep up the Teesta Valley on the route of the pre-war Everest expeditions. We stopped frequently for tea and Sikkimese cherry brandy, which has a pleasant flavour and a powerful kick. For the first twenty miles we followed the river in dense jungle through a narrow gorge that opened out into a wide and fertile valley terraced for paddy. An abundance of fruit trees was beginning to flower. Towards the head of the valley the road began to climb steadily for three thousand feet to Gangtok, perched in a commanding position above us. Prayer flags lined the road like a triumphal way to this fairyland town, little larger than Kalimpong and reminiscent of a Swiss alpine village.

Above the town on an open space with uninterrupted views in all directions, lies the Palace where the Maharaja of Sikkim lives with his American-born queen. Sikkim is an independent kingdom like Bhutan.

I was fortunate in meeting a friendly police officer who showed me the chancery building. It stands surrounded by wide lawns in front of the Maharaja's Palace and is both the gompa, or temple, for the Maharaja and the parliament. Lamas were making a circuit of the flagstones below the massive white walls of the gompa telling their beads, a pleasant form of relaxation and exercise in the warm morning sun. The building was of Tibetan character, having a low-pitched roof and overhanging eaves, the corners of which were gently curved upwards; some fine carving and paintings decorated the inside of the temple. Wandering through the gardens we nearly tripped over a junior constable snoozing under a bush, his rifle propped against his knee. He was roundly upbraided by his superior and sent off at a run with several ideas on how to mend his ways.

I walked down the hill through a forest of prayer flags towards the Institute of Tibetology; many priceless books salvaged from the recent onslaught of the Cultural Revolution across the northern border are available there for lamas and scholars to study in pleasant and peaceful surroundings. On a hill a little distant stood a large white chorten beside a monastery; beautiful red flowers were blooming on the trees and bananas ripening into fruit; a group of gardeners were playing dice in the shade of a magnolia tree, two young lamas watching intently over their shoulders.

I went slowly back into the bazaar enjoying the tranquillity. I wished to buy a Tibetan carpet, but few are available nowadays; the refugees either sold them in the early days after their escape or, having come to understand their value, are sensibly hanging on to them against a more auspicious day. After much searching I bought a beautiful small carpet; the background was a deep russet, the other colours were orange, turquoise and apple green. Two dragons and two phoenixes filled each quadrant pointing towards a central all-seeing eye and the border was composed of symbolic clouds and rain.

On the evening I returned from Gangtok I was talking with Mingma Tshering, the Sherpa sirdar on all of Hillary's expeditions, and learnt with great sadness of the death, at the age of twenty-one, of Dakya Sherpa, who had helped us to explore Hiunchuli Patan in West Nepal in 1962. I questioned Mingma exhaustively to make sure we were talking about the same man – so many Sherpas, Tibetans and Bhutanese have but one single name that confusion arises unless one also knows the name of their village. But sadly there was no doubt and we felt deeply empty at the loss of our friend; when the other boys flagged during our desperate winter-beating journey round Dhaulagiri, Dakya never complained and shared the loads to his own disadvantage; at each

43

midday halt he used to wash Sarah's underwear and hang it on a line to dry; he was a combination of phenomenal strength and gentleness. He had been taken to the Gurkha hospital in Dharan, where he died, having probably suffered an acute attack of tuberculosis, that scourge of the hills.

Sarah's permit had still not arrived and we decided I should go into Bhutan before my own expired, so that I could begin the medical work and try to expedite her entry. Lakpa Doma was proving such a help with the children that I felt less worried about leaving Sarah alone with them. Sarah's command of Nepali language was rusty from disuse but was coming back with the aid of a small dictionary and phrase book prepared for the Gurkha soldiers. Such commonly used phrases as "What is that man doing behind that bushy-topped tree?" or "Your rifle is not clean today," were of little use to her. But these books compared favourably with an American missionary text we also possessed with such verbal abusage as "Real nice potatoes can be gotten in the market."

In the mornings Lakpa did the washing and then she entertained Judith, with whom her patience was inexhaustible; so Sarah was free in the afternoons, which would be more important later as she intended to help me with clinics and my research work.

Together we visited Rani Chuni, mother of the Queen of Bhutan, at her house in Kalimpong. Remembering our disastrous royal tea party in Calcutta, we waited in her flower filled garden where the children could run about freely. A few moments later a small, frail-looking woman of seventy appeared in gardening trousers. She excused herself in order to change and some moments later appeared in her chuba and made us welcome.

She told us that her late husband had also been a keen gardener in Bhutan, where he introduced apples, many plants and varieties of corn and trout, into their home village of Ha. Her face showed little of the sadness she has suffered in recent years. Rani Chuni was a daughter of the Maharaja of Sikkim. She married Raja Sonam Tobgyal Dorji, the prime minister of Bhutan, and they lived in the valley of Ha, east of Paro, and they also owned this house in Kalimpong. On Raja Dorji's death in

44

1953 his eldest son Jigme succeeded as prime minister. Jigme Dorji was assassinated in April 1964, so bringing to an end the close liaison of the royal family and the Dorji family, who had ruled Bhutan together for more than fifty years.

Rani Chuni displayed a deep affection and sympathy for her people in Bhutan where she used to ride for miles on a bicycle from her dispensary at Namseyling in the Thimphu Valley, visiting patients. She spoke perfect English with barely a trace of accent and her knowledge, from personal experience of worldwide travelling with her husband, was encyclopaedic.

So I took the "Bhutan Bus" from Kalimpong bound for Phuntsoling, leaving Sarah and the children to follow as soon as their permit arrived. Sarah had made so many friends I knew she would not be lonely and would be well cared for by the sisters at the Himalayan Hotel. We dropped to the Teesta Khola again, level with the plains, and then drove for miles through the Dooars, a rich tea-growing area that reaches Bhutan's southern border. To my left I could see the foothills of Bhutan rising steeply; I felt the intense excitement of knowing that I would soon set foot on the soil of the country of which I had dreamed so much during the past four years.

Paro Dzong

## CHAPTER 5

Phuntsoling is the roadhead for the single highway that penetrates the west of Bhutan to reach the two main towns – Thimphu, the capital, and Paro. Another road two hundred miles to the east goes in to Tashigang. Until seven years ago Phuntsoling was a village composed of a few shacks standing beside the river on the narrow spit of flat land between the Bhutanese foothills and the Indian Dooars. Formerly more mules than men were to be seen there because Phuntsoling was the starting point of the main mule and pony route, by which all trade and traffic passed into Bhutan. Then the journey to Thimphu took seven days. Phuntsoling is now a busy, corrugated-iron shanty town with a thriving bazaar and has become the hub of all communications between India and West Bhutan since the building of the road in 1962. The town accommodates the district administration, postal and telegraph communications, units of the army, road engineers and government transport. I was housed in the state guest house on instructions from Thimphu, an honour I gratefully accepted but felt was far beyond my station.

Next morning a jeep arrived to take me to Paro. I was told

this was part of my "programme" and I would shortly afterwards move over to Thimphu for an audience with the King, who was at that moment away hunting near Punakha. Not far distant I could see the zig-zag of the road scarring the hillside and rising through the foothills, which abut sharply on to the plains. After less than a mile we began to climb a metalled stretch of road through thick Terai jungle and were soon looking down on a rolling sea of tree tops. Below, the plains stretched away into a haze on the distant horizon intersected by many rivers, which drained from the mountains and sparkled with the sun's reflection.

After following the crest of a spur the road took to the mountain and rose more than 4,000 feet by a series of long bends. The people in these southern hills of Bhutan are almost exclusively Nepalis who migrated several generations ago after disastrous floods in East Nepal to work at rubber tapping. They have taken Bhutanese citizenship but have retained their Hindu religion and Nepalese customs and dress. The major part of the labour force maintaining the road built by Indian army engineers are Nepalis recruited from outside Bhutan.

Scores of women squatted at the roadside breaking up stones with heavy hammers, holding a metal ring in their left hand to prevent the shattered fragments from flying away. Small children laboriously built the broken stones into straight-sided piles three feet square and one foot high; mothers placed their babies in cradles made from cardboard boxes, under the shade of umbrellas resting open on the ground; young girls, hardly more than children, carried baskets of stones and soil supported by headbands; the men laid the stones and rolled them flat, spreading tar on the surface. These labour gangs were colourful and full of life and chatter despite the tedium of the work and the low wages they earned. The road was similar to the Tribuvan Rajpath which leads in to Kathmandu but was more precipitous and winding.

Eventually we reached a crest at 7,200 feet and looked up the long, deep valley of the Wong Chhu which drains from Paro and Thimphu. Dense jungle gave way to pine forest; there was a uniformity and softness of the rolling ridges covered with trees

47

from mountain top to river bed. The road wound in and out following the contours of land; an unbroken drop from the outside edge gave a more horrifying sensation of verticality than any other mountain road I have been on.

In the shade lay icy slush where snow had failed to melt and I felt the impact of intensely cold air. The plains were no longer visible but the dusty haze that rises from them was apparent in the distance; snow-flecked hilltops lay to the north but no high mountains could be seen.

After midday we arrived at Chhukha bridge, the halfway mark, and passed the police check. Temporary bamboo-matting shacks of the roadworkers' camps and an occasional farm were the only evidence of habitation. I felt I was entering the Interior, for these deep, forested valleys and high hills have indeed acted as Bhutan's natural defensive barrier in time past, keeping the outside world in general, and enemies in particular, at bay.

Our driver was a pleasant fellow and gave no cause for anxiety; we stopped at a road house for a rest and a meal of Tibetan momo, noodles and tea. The middle section of road was largely unmetalled and seemed to hang on loose shale and mud. We gradually dropped to the river again and travelled along a narrow gorge, which heightened the feeling of penetrating the final rampart of this natural fortress. At the confluence of the Paro Chhu and the Thimphu Chhu we turned left. The forest receded and we were now surrounded by barren brown hillsides transformed into rich gold by the soft evening light. Small castle fortresses, called dzongs, appeared at strategic points commanding extensive views from their hilltop positions. My excitement began to rise as I felt I was entering the real Bhutan. The road followed close to the river, which was deep, fast-flowing and clear as crystal; the mountains were far enough away for the glacial mud and silt that so discolours Alpine rivers to have settled. I was told the rivers were full of trout, stocked many years ago from Kashmir.

Quite suddenly the valley opened out with flat paddy fields and farms; long sloping hillsides thinly covered with pinewoods lay on both sides. The houses stood in isolated groups of two or

48

three built of sturdy construction with packed earth ground floors, wooden upper floors and low-pitched, slatted wooden roofs.

I was anxious lest darkness might have fallen by the time we reached Paro but on turning a corner I saw a magnificent sight before me in the twilight. On a hill above the town, where lights now sparkled, stood the massive white walls of Paro Dzong rising from solid rock foundations like a diminutive Potala Palace in Lhasa. I could see no details in the darkness, which enhanced the beauty of this fantastic fairyland stronghold, making all the mysteries I had ever dreamed about Tibet and Bhutan become vividly alive. I have never seen such an enchanted place.

I reached the guest house, tired after the eight-hour journey buffeting and bumping in a poorly sprung jeep. Dr. Wangdi Zangpo, a Sikkimese working in the government medical service, warmly welcomed me and ordered Yanku, the boy assigned to look after me, to cook a meal.

I went to bed wearing my quilted down jacket and all my clothes inside my sleeping bag because of the intense cold. I lay awake with the flood of recent experiences cascading through my head and the exciting prospect before me of exploring Paro in detail next day.

The morning was clear and the warm sunshine most welcome after the coldness of the night. On the verandah of the guest house overlooking the valley I breakfasted with Dr. George Eberle, a Swiss veterinary surgeon, who was investigating tapeworm infestation of yaks and dogs. Paro Dzong stood on the opposite side of the valley commanding every aspect of the dwellings and fields that lay below it. An ancient circular watchtower with a high vantage point looked out over the main dzong, acting as a retreat should the dzong fall into the hands of the enemy. The dzong's white walls sloped gently upwards towards a wide surmounting roof, whose eaves overhung the carved and painted windows in the upper part. In the middle of the square court stood another taller building with a gold ornamental cupola crowning its wide roof.

The river flowed close under the walls of the dzong and was

crossed by a covered and fortified cantilever bridge. Groves of willow trees grew in the meadow surrounding the Queen's Palace. The valley spread away in two directions and was mazed in an irregular pattern with rice fields, some of which were flooded in preparation for planting while others were studded with the stubble of last year's harvest. Small clusters of houses and farms were scattered through the length and breadth of this fertile valley, which divided above the strategic bottleneck where the dzong lay; two branches diverging north-west and northwards led towards Chomolhari and the pass to Phari in the Chumbi Valley. On the wooded hilltops, much denuded for building materials and fuel, I saw many small monasteries and chorten. Everywhere from valley floor to mountain top prayer flags waved "om manis" heavenwards. We sat quietly tasting the pleasure afforded by this unique view which has changed little since a Jesuit priest, Cacella, described it three hundred and fifty years ago:

"The town of Pargao lies in a beautiful, wide plain which extends very pleasantly between two mountain ranges. Just then the fields were covered with very promising crops of wheat and rice. Two rivers divide the plain, and lend it freshness and beauty, especially through the large willow-trees and the many irrigation-canals that emanate from the rivers. The houses begin at the very edge of the plain, large, high buildings with very thick walls, generally of three, four and even five stories, greatly beautified by windows and verandahs. These houses, however, do not line up into streets, rather they are sprinkled all over the plain and along the foot of the mountains. Thus they form a town of such length that the part of it which we saw and traversed must be at least three leagues, and there still remained something to be seen. For the plain continues in the way I have said till it comes to a mountain ridge which splits it lengthwise, and from which on either side descend the streams that water it. The town creeps up these slopes in two large stretches, the ends of which pass a good way beyond the two rivers. We arrived in this town on March 25th, 1627."

Dasho Sangey Dorji, the Paro Dronyer and director of administration who looks after guests and the guest house, arrived and sat with us; he was a large friendly man with a deep voice and humorous chuckle. He had arranged that I should spend the morning visiting the dzong with Dr. George Eberle and his assistant Dorji Tsering, who worked in the animal husbandry department. Dorji spoke good English and was naturally courteous and keen to answer our questions, though his replies often appeared biased by a burning patriotism or an urgent desire to please. Traditional oriental acquiescence becomes infuriating when replies are made according to the answer expected to give most pleasure or cause least offence; of this, Dorji was a master, nearly driving George Eberle to distraction when accurate answers were required in his veterinary work.

We passed through the bazaar where a few small shops flanked a wide street down which laden ponies ambled, their neck bells making pleasant music in the still morning air. A long gallery raised above the packed earth of the street allowed us to look in through the open windows of the shops at merchandise displayed on shelves. We could not walk round the shop but rather stood at the window and pointed out any articles we wished to buy; these were limited to cheap goods from India, cooking pots and utensils, locally sewn clothing and a few tins of food. Some itinerant Tibetans had set up their wares on the ground and were carrying on trade. I foresaw that we should do the main shopping for our journey at Phuntsoling where the selection was greater than in Paro.

Walking towards the dzong we reached the archery ground; teams were assembling for a match, which we intended to watch later in the morning. Further on was a row of large white chortens raised on square plinths, in the heart of which certain holy scriptures were said to be walled up. A stream had been diverted to run beside the walls of the palace, where it raced and bubbled through groves of willow trees, naked in the winteriness of January.

We reached the river that flowed lazily beside the walls of the dzong. A gate-tower stood on either bank with a heavy timber door through which we had to pass to reach the bridge. The towers acted both as a fortification guarding the entrance to the bridge and also as a counterweight over the piers from whence sprang three rows of cantilevers, each row with four enormous timbers two feet square projecting beyond the row below. The original width of the gap to be spanned was about fifty feet, now reduced to twenty feet between the furthest projecting cantilevers. We later saw this skilled engineering principle applied to many bridges and buildings in Bhutan. No metal nails or screws were used, all the joints being of tenon and mortise or dove-tailed with wooden pins to secure adjacent timbers.

Some elderly ladies, warmed by a shaft of sunlight entering the porch, were gossiping while spinning wool; their children were turning the prayer wheels recessed into the walls as fast as they would go, making a crunching mechanical noise. The bridge had a high balustrade supporting a roof over its entire length, not so much for the comfort of its users as to protect the wood from the weather, which would otherwise shorten its life span. Elaborate decorations painted round the portals gave a touch of artistry to a beautiful construction.

We climbed gently through avenues of trees across sloping lawns below the walls of the dzong towering over us. Long slits in the lowermost part below the high mounted windows lit the dungeons; of these Dorji spoke with awe but was unforthcoming on any details of the present inmates. In the courtyard before the wide staircase leading up to the main door we halted for Dorji to put on his kabney, the ceremonial white scarf that must be worn by all men on entering the dzong; about twelve feet long and two feet wide, it is wound on in a special fashion: beginning over the left shoulder it is draped across the body, round the back, over the shoulder and then is hooked over the first free end and thrown backwards over the shoulder again. The scarf is used when making a ceremonial bow but is of much greater service in carrying a bundle of luggage; whether for children or firewood, the Bhutanese prefer the kabney to the Nepali coolie's basket. A tall prayer flag stood in the centre of the yard, beyond which a long flight of stairs passed through mighty, studded wooden doors into a dark corridor, which turned left for about twenty feet and opened by another doorway

52

on to the inner courtyard. The change in direction of the entrance passage would make storming of the gates more difficult, this being the only access to the dzong, other than attempting to scale a hundred feet of the bare outside walls to reach window level.

In the centre of the inner courtyard stood a building higher than the outer walls – a dzong within a dzong, with ferocious dragons' heads carved at the corners of the overhanging roofs which were made of split pine shingles weighted with heavy stones. Besides being carpenters and architects of great skill, the Bhutanese are passionately fond of colour; roof eaves and window frames are decorated with painted designs and figures of animals. Paints are made from various coloured earths boiled with certain vegetable roots to form a thick gum, creating tones varying from grey through ochre to rich red; vegetable dyes and indigo are also used. The resulting colours weather if exposed to the rain; wide eaves, characteristic of all Bhutanese buildings, throw water from the roof well clear of the walls and protect the paintings from fading or running. The space immediately under the roof is open, providing a wide gap above the uppermost story; in domestic houses this space is used as a loft for cattle fodder, its structural function being to allow free circulation of the wind, which daily blows with tremendous force and if enclosed would form pressure pockets and lift off the low-pitched roof.

Long, open galleries faced on to the courtyard, off which led various offices and apartments. One corner more ornate than the rest was set aside for the King's state rooms, where he stays on visits from Thimphu. As women are banished from the dzong precincts after sunset, the Queen stays in her palace across the river. A crowd of poor people and Tibetan refugees were being fed by the lamas, who are of the Red Sect of Buddhism and wore red robes with saffron coloured shirts, adding a vivid dash of colour to the already gaudy painting of the galleries. Chained in one corner were two small Himalayan bears, recently caught by the King while hunting. We were taken through every corner of the dzong, impressive in its beauty and serenity.

At the door of the main gompa, or temple, we were met by the head lama, a frail man of about seventy with a balding head,

Wall-building, Thimphu Dzong
Thimphu Bazaar

small moustache and a heavily lined face. From the folds of his cloak he produced a square silver box beautifully worked and gilded. He chose an unblemished pan leaf from several in the box and tore it gently in two; under the dark green leaves he thumbed over various pieces of betel nut until he found one to his liking and split it with a penknife; he then replaced the box in his cloak and produced a circular silver box similarly engraved. With slow ceremony he dipped the pan leaf into a white lime paste, spreading it thinly, and carefully wrapped the betel nut in the leaf, which he passed to me. I placed it discreetly in my cheek and chewed slowly; bitter juices began to flow. The exchange of pan and betel is an honoured custom at all levels of society from kings and princes to passing wayfarers and peasants. A bright red stain discolours the teeth of habitual chewers and red gobs of spittle soil the floors and pavements. The Bhutanese are reputed for their addiction to the betel nut, which is a stimulant drug; I found myself feeling quite light-headed after chewing for a short while so I rapidly expelled my gob in traditional fashion.

Half a dozen gaylongs, or young monks in training, hung behind the head lama and peered at us. We entered the hall of the gompa, the walls of which were covered in paintings depicting the life of Buddha. Young gaylongs, some only seven or eight years old, were chanting and playing drums and long horns under the tuition of a senior monk. Beyond was the hall where the National Assembly is held. Finally we entered an inner sanctuary where sat a statue of Buddha thirty feet high surrounded by many smaller deities adopting erotic and warlike postures.

From my description the reader will have learnt a certain amount about the appearance and function of Paro Dzong, typical of many dzongs across the country. But I must enlarge on this to complete the picture of the dzong, which physically and metaphorically dominates every aspect of life, temporal and spiritual, for persons of all strata in the society of Bhutan.

The dzong is the civic and religious centre of each region. The largest, from west to east, are Ha, Paro, Thimphu, Lingshi, Punakha, Wangdu Phodrang, Tongsa, Byakar, Shemgang, Mongar, Lhuntsi, Tashi-Yangtsi and Tashigang. In former days the regions were governed by penlops or dzongpens' independent princelings often warring with each other. The civil administration nowadays comes under two principal officers: first the thrimpon, second the nyerchen.

The thrimpon is the regional governor directly answerable to the King, who is head of state. He controls local government, acts as magistrate in legal cases, commands the police and administers the district organisation. At village level the headmen are the gaps (or mundels in the south) and their assistants, the cheupens; a number of gaps are under a dumpa, responsible to the thrimpon. One man from every village is appointed in rotation by the gap to be on duty in the dzong, a responsibility he may hold for a month or more. He acts as a messenger and goes between the dzong and the village to arrange the business of compulsory government labour or carries edicts from the central government. In this way the chain of communication from government to the people, especially now that most dzongs have radio stations, is quick despite the country's geography, so opposed to speed.

The nyerchen is the quartermaster dealing with government finances, accounts and taxes. The latter are often paid in kind and the large store-rooms and granaries in the dzong supply food to the lamas, the police and the army. The thrimpon's assistant is the ramjan; a large number of clerks and orderlies staff the various offices.

The title Dasho is given to anyone in high office in Bhutan. A high-ranking dasho is distinguished by his magenta dzong scarf and, hanging by his side, a three-foot-long sword with an embossed silver handle and scabbard, presented to him by the King.

In religious life the dzong acts as a monastery to house the lamas. At Punakha Dzong lives the most senior and powerful abbot, the Bhutanese equivalent of the Tibetan Dalai Lama. The head lama of the dzong, the omze, is assisted by a lopon kudung in charge of discipline; the champen instructs gaylongs in dances, music, reading and writing. Young boys are put into religious training by their families who thus acquire spiritual merit; they may leave before their final vows if they are found unsuitable or if they do not like the life, which has many of the unpleasant features of our boarding schools.

Above the regional administration is the National Assembly which meets at Paro twice each year. To the Assembly come the central government ministers and all the thrimpons, nyerchens subdivisional officers and delegates of the people – a long trek every six months for those from the more distant dzongs. The King, or Gyelpo as he is called in Bhutanese, presides but has no direct say in the government, although his influence is crucial Immediately below the King is the commander-in-chief of the army, the chief secretary and deputy chief secretary. The central government has eight ministers, chosen by the King, and the secretary general, in charge of the development wing concerned with departments of geology, forestry, education, agriculture health, animal husbandry, engineering and the postal system.

I have elaborated these details in order to emphasise the degree of organisation within this small country, which has emerged from a mediaeval era during the past decade and whose civil service, by any standards, is highly efficient.

After completing our tour we climbed the hill behind the dzong to the ancient circular fortress, its upper part indented as if a half slice had been cut from a cake. Work was in progress to restore the building as a museum. We looked out over the roofs of the dzong and away up the Paro Valley; being mid-winter, the dominant colours in the valley floor were brown, ochre and yellow, but later in the year when the willows are in leaf and the rice shoots come through, a rich emerald green gives a softer appearance.

On a distant hill a column of smoke rose from a forest fire; as heavy fines are imposed on the owner according to the area of destruction a communal effort is made to quell such a blaze. Descending the hill we passed a long house on whose door was chalked "Paro Primary School".

My feelings about the day are summed up by Lord Ronaldshay who visited Paro in 1921:

"... We found ourselves, as though caught up on some magic time machine fitted fantastically with a reverse, flung back across the centuries into the feudalism of a middle age."

Archery

## CHAPTER 6

Returning to the river we crossed the bridge and found the archery match well under way. The archery ground was situated beside the large chortens; willow trees grew down either side forming a wide avenue about one hundred and fifty yards long. Archery is the national sport of Bhutan and, like sports elsewhere in the world, has a fanatical following tantamount to a religion. The match had started early in the morning and continued without interruption, except for drinks of chang, and cold rice brought out by the women, until it was too dark to see the target.

Two teams, each of about half a dozen men, shot down the ground towards the targets, one foot wide and three feet high set on a raised ramp at either end. Each pair of archers shot off against each other; then they walked to the target end to act as markers for their fellows. Everyone having shot, they collected up their arrows and shot back in the reverse direction: so it went on, to and fro, all day long. Spectators squatted in the shade of the willows or followed the archers, closely studying form. Nearby a stream flowed to a water mill whence came the sound of grinding corn; some women were winnowing chaff from the grain in the light breeze.

Bows are made of split bamboo about six feet in length; shredded nettle stalks, twisted, folded on each other, and twisted again, make the strings, which are kept wet in order to maintain their maximum tension; arrows of slender bamboo are feathered and tipped with metal. The archers use leather finger guards because the pull on the string requires great strength and a long day's shooting causes soreness of the finger pulps.

Intense concentration contorted the faces of the bowmen standing with feet placed at right angles, the grimace intensified as the pull on the string tightened and then broke into a broad smile as the arrow cleft the air with a soft whistle. Loud yells sped the arrow on its way and vociferous oaths were uttered when it became apparent that the flight path was not on target. A good shot was greeted with ecstatic shouts and a triumphant dance, the men circling very slowly, bows held at arm's length while performing a graceful motion of the hands and feet. The markers waited on the ramp beside the targets in direct line of fire pointing with their bows to where the arrows landed or indicating with special signs where it had overshot or fallen short.

The target was hit only half a dozen times in the day, but on each occasion shrieks of mirth and acclaim rent the air and play completely stopped as spectators and players danced and congratulated one another. Each team brought its own dancing girls dressed in their best kira, who performed and sang quite unconcerned in the middle of the ground with the arrows whistling over their heads. Only once in our time in Bhutan did I see someone scarred from an arrow injury.

The picturesque setting was enriched by the dress of the participants, which intensified the atmosphere of mediaeval pageantry. An unwritten law of the country, encouraged by the King, prescribes that Drukpa – the true Bhutanese – should wear national dress. Western clothing is discouraged except among the Nepali Drukpa and foreigners. Men wear the ko (or boku as it is commonly known, using a Tibetan word). When first put on it falls like a long dressing gown to the feet; the edges are grasped, held sidewards and both are folded to meet in the small of the back. By a series of wriggling contortions the whole garment is raised, keeping the original folds, until the lower edge is level with the knee and looks like a kilt. A woven belt wound several times round the waist secures it tightly and forms a voluminous pouch in front. The sleeves are long and loose; a white shirt appears in loose folds at the neck and at the wrist is turned over making a cuff, the length of which denotes the social importance of the wearer. Although complicated to arrange it is a practical garment as the pouch stores a man's pan-leaf boxes, purse and drinking bowl, and a knife is thrust into his belt. In winter breeches are worn under the ko tucked into long socks with leather shoes.

Although the style is uniform the colours and patterns of weave are varied and rarely does one ko match another. Some machine-made materials are imported from India, but the more decorative cloth is hand-woven. Looms are found in the porch of every home, whence comes the clackety-clack of the weaving stick and treadle.

The Bhutanese appearance is Mongoloid by contrast to the Indo-Aryan features of the plainsmen to the south of the great mountain range, and the Bhutanese are more powerfully built than their Himalayan neighbours.

Men wear their hair short; small moustaches grow at the outer corner of their upper lip and curl round the edge of the mouth; occasionally they have small goatee beards. Facial hair is sparse and they sit for hours with tweezers and a broken fragment of mirror plucking out offending hairs. The men are handsome with solid, well defined bone structure, narrow eyes and thin lips. Whereas these features suit the male, women suffer by them and are rarely beautiful; heavy, rounded faces are poorly set off by severe close-cropped hair and fringe. A life of heavy labour tends to obscure their feminine attractions and makes them compare unfavourably with their more graceful sisters from Nepal and India. Their dress, the kira, is a single piece of woven cloth put on somewhat like a Grecian costume and held at each shoulder by circular silver buckles three inches in diameter. The women's woven belt makes a less capacious pouch than that of the men, yet their feminine figures are obscured and appear shapeless.

Almost on the stroke of noon the wind rose and turned the calm air into a dust storm; it continued to blow and died as quickly as it had come at about four o'clock. I had experienced such a wind before in the north of Nepal at Muktinath and Jomosom, which lie in the Trans-Himalaya and have a climate typical of Tibet. An extraordinary cloud pattern formed over the summit of Dhaulagiri at midday, one cloud assuming the shape of a hovering angel or a swooping bird when the wind began to blow. Similar windstorms are often referred to in literature on Tibet and may account for the people's high-coloured cheeks and weather-beaten faces. In late afternoon when the falling sun was obscured by cloud the wind became raw and I preferred not to venture outside.

My programme to move to Thimphu was suddenly altered and Dr. Zangpo, who appeared to be in charge, told me I would stay in Paro a few days longer. He demanded frequent reassurance and appreciation, concluding every statement with the words,"I do very nicely, huh?" He was a shy, nervous little Sikkimese man who had spent many years as a doctor attached to various diplomatic missions; for twelve years he lived in Lhasa and was turned out during the Sino-Indian war of 1962. His description of the behaviour of the aggressors towards the Tibetans was horrifying and amply supported the use of that emotionally charged word genocide.

Dr. Zangpo was also physician to the Queen in Paro. At the end of one day when escorting a royal picnic party as the attendant physician he became lost, so delaying the Queen's return to her palace; eventually he was discovered in a meadow hunting for frogs' legs to cook for his supper.

By contrast Dasho Sangey Dorji, the genial administrator, was large and benign; he was an attentive host and often came to call on George Eberle and me in the guest house. He spoke reasonable English intersposed with quaint, inapposite phrases and idioms, which caused us much mirth. He held court in his office, seated behind a big desk surrounded by a barricade of folders, firmly and appropriately bound up with fading red tape. Suppliant

Chhimi at Wangdu Phodrang

clerks and anxious civil servants came to and fro with pathetic little petitions, opening thus: "Most respected and honourable Dasho, my earnest prayer is that your humble servant may . . ." He dealt with each case in a sympathetic and fatherly manner, adding some quip of worldly wisdom to his judgment. Dasho Sangey suggested I should visit Dukye Dzong and Taktsang Gompa; he ordered Yangku, the cook boy, to prepare some food and to accompany me.

Dukye lies ten miles up the Paro Valley; the dzong, now ruined by fire, is perched on top of a rocky promontory at a point where the valley narrows. Its strategic position guards entry to Bhutan by the Tremo La pass from Phari, which lies on the Lhasa road between Yatung and Gyantse in the Chumbi Valley of Tibet. Before reaching Dukye a susidiary peak of Chomolhari called Chotarkay came into view, its radiant white snows filling the head of the valley.

I explored the ruins of the fortress and noted a feature I saw elsewhere only at Byakar Dzong: a double wall enclosing a passage led from the fort down the hill to the bank of the river on the far side of the valley, small towers were built at intervals and the passage in former days was roofed. This complete barrier across the valley provided a way for safely bringing reinforcements to the towers, a means of covered retreat to the safety of the dzong above and access to a water supply in time of siege.

I climbed a hill behind Dukye to look for wider views. After an hour my companion, Yangku, showed signs of wear and puzzlement at my wishing to make so apparently pointless a pilgrimage. He needed little persuasion to go down and I continued for another hour until I came to a place where I had a magnificent view of Chomolhari, a fine looking peak with gentle, fluted ridges climbed by Spencer Chapman and Pasang Dawa in 1937. I was walking in thick woods and, on hearing the loud crack of a branch ahead, I turned and fled. The previous day I had seen a man whose face was badly scarred from mauling by a bear; I did not stop to verify this figment of my imagination, the mere suggestion was sufficient to hasten me down the hill.

The following day we started early for Taktsang Monastery, arriving after a two and a half hour climb through pleasant pine

Sarah removing Judith's nits
Adam in harness, with bear

forest that smelt sweetly of resin. Yangku sniffed and spat continuously as if to ease the pressure on his lungs, but was tolerably content when he realised he need not carry a load.

"Last time I come here, I come on horse," he assured me. "Dasho ride on horse." I realised that horse riding carries much prestige in Bhutan and I was considered odd for not availing myself of it.

From a vantage point on the ridge I saw a number of shrines precariously situated on the hill opposite; one in particular appeared to cling to the side of an enormous vertical cliff. It gains its name, Taktsang, meaning the tiger's lair, from ancient legend. Many centuries ago a tiger flew over the mountains from Tibet carrying on its back a holy lama who became the abbot of Taktsang. He reputedly brought Buddhism to Bhutan by founding the Drukpa sect.

We climbed for lunch to a monastery, now being restored by the Queen and met a three-year-old incarnate Lama Rimpoche, being brought up under the care of his parents in this mountain retreat until old enough to be formally educated. He was discovered by various mystical portents confirmed with obscure tests of genuineness by senior lamas sent into the country on the quest for the reincarnation of a former Guru Rimpoche. He was a dear little boy, full of fun and mischief; it seemed sad that he should be committed so young to this ascetic life, but oriental traditions and beliefs are beyond the understanding of Westerners.

While touring the temple we were joined by three cheerful Bhutanese men making a pilgrimage of all the shrines in the region involving several days' journey and rewarded by much religious merit. They carried a large tin of cooking fat, which they melted for oil to light lamps in front of the altars of fearsome gods surrounding the Lord Buddha. One was a sinister, brigand-like fellow with a moustache, his face half wreathed in a scarf to protect an aching tooth; the other two were younger and grinned cheerfully, cracking jokes at their companion's plight.

My fellow travellers moved with speed and agility on the descent and I was hard pressed to keep up. From a mani prayer wall we looked across a deep ravine to Taktsang Monastery built on a ledge on the vertical face of a thousand-foot granite cliff. The engineering skill involved in building such a nest of temples in this sensational position was highly developed. The situation was doubtless conducive to meditation and disposal of refuse was evidently no problem. We followed a narrow path into the gulley where a large waterfall had eroded a channel; crossing over the chasm by a slippery log bridge under the spray of the cascade we climbed a flight of a hundred narrow steps cut from solid rock and overhanging a stupendous drop. I breathed a sigh of relief on entering the gate of the monastery, inside which were many rooms exquisitely painted with scenes of Buddha's life. An old janitor monk sat in the sun in a small courtyard telling his beads, oblivious of his airy position.

We descended rapidly from Taktsang and my friends expressed surprise that a stranger could keep up their pace; they shared Yanku's opinion that foreigners, like dashos, always travel in jeeps or on horseback – never on foot. On the pleasant walk down the road to Paro we passed a pilgrim on his way to Taktsang; he was covering the distance by laying himself on the ground, making a mark at arm's length, then getting up, standing on the mark and repeating the process. For protection he wore a leather apron, leather shields on his knees and a pair of wooden boards on his hands. He had spent several months already on the road from Punakha and we guessed he would take a further three or four weeks to reach Taktsang. However, the religious merit acquired by such devotion should assure him a suitable reincarnation.

Our road passed through several villages with houses grouped at random surrounded by fields. Bhutanese houses are solidly built, varying little in style across the country. The ground floor is used as a cattle stable and has unfaced walls of hard packed mud; the walls of the upper two or three floors have limewashed plaster panels between supporting beams. Bay windows have twelve, sixteen or twenty openings, each about a foot square; these are rounded above, each having its own individual sliding wooden shutter. The low-pitched roof of pine slats is weighted with large round stones from the river; as in the dzong, the open loft is used for fodder storage. The houses are solid and dignified, showing a high standard of craftsmanship in architectural construction; the

63

artistic decoration of frames and lintels is as intricate as work of the Newar carpenters and woodcarvers of Kathmandu and Patan in Nepal.

In the evening Dasho Dawa Tsering, the secretary general, arranged a dinner for me to which many of the Paro dignitaries were invited; I was deeply honoured by his hospitality. He was a young man who was educated at school in Darjeeling, later studied law in Calcutta and has travelled all over the world as Bhutan's representative on the Colombo Plan. Best Scotch whisky flowed freely, enhancing an interesting and convivial evening; also it was a personal celebration as news had arrived that Sarah had received her permit and expected to join me later in the week.

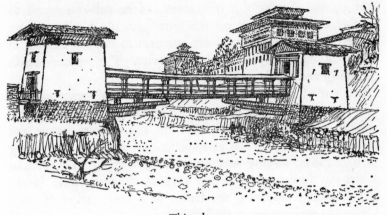

Thimphu

## CHAPTER 7

The journey to Thimphu took four hours by jeep. We retraced
our road to the confluence and followed the Wong Chhu
northwards; above Simtokha Dzong the valley widened but was
less beautiful than Paro. At Thimphu a dzong and a city are
being built on open farmland to become the administrative
capital of Bhutan. The seat of royalty used to be in Bumthang
but the King has now built a palace at Dechen Chholing, three
miles up the valley from the new dzong, now being constructed
round the ancient Tashichho Dzong – "the fortress of the glorious
religion". Thimphu Dzong is approaching completion; at
the four corners stand massive towers, each a separate palace
for the King, the commander-in-chief of the army, the head lama
and the monks. The outside walls complete a hollow square
three hundred feet in length and house the offices of various
government departments, having a similar gigantic appearance
to the Escorial in Madrid. Every stone block has been hand-
chiselled and every timber beam cut and trimmed with adze and
axe by the two thousand strong labour force permanently working on its construction and living in a shanty town across the
river. By a system of compulsory labour each family in
Bhutan must provide one person to work for one month each

year on the dzong; this obligation can be sub-contracted to another family if work on the farm prevents a man leaving home. It is not uncommon for one man to stay six months in Thimphu doing several people's service. The system works efficiently and is fair and reasonable.

Inside the main court of the dzong a human historical pageant that could have taken place in the building of our mediaeval cathedrals, unfolded before me. An old master mason and carpenter with no formal architectural training was supervising various gangs; twenty men were manoeuvring an enormous square-cut timber with ropes; masons chiselled stone blocks in one corner preparing the facing to a new section of wall. Under the supervision of the head gardener a band of girls were carrying baskets of wood chippings from the timber mill below the dzong to spread on the newly-dug rose beds beside the King's apartment. When the chippings were burned to make ash for fertiliser a pall of smoke hung above the dzong, which appeared to be on fire.

Young girls were packing down mud in a wooden mould of boards, four feet long and two feet square, to make the thick foundation walls similar to those of the domestic houses. Six girls with heavy pounding-rods climbed on to the mould and, shuffling slowly round in a dancing rhythm accompanied by singing, trampled the firm mud dug from a nearby quarry until it was packed solid. Fifty girls made a spectacular sight silhouetted against the skyline as they stamped one of the high inner walls of the dzong.

In one part of the dzong the carpenter's work was finished and the painters were working on the interior decoration. In a shed at the back paints were being prepared; buckets of different richly coloured earths were standing beside large vats in which a root was boiling. After several hours of this treatment the liquid was allowed to cool to a semi-solid gum; earth and gum were mixed in chosen proportions making a paint of the requisite shade. Fine chalk in a cloth bag was then banged on a paper stencil with holes punched along the lines, leaving a dotted chalk imprint on the wood when the paper was removed. A wild looking young man of about twenty with long hair and artistic features was executing perfect freehand drawings of dragons, phoenixes and other exotic beasts, while the pastel colouring was completed by an assistant.

I stayed in a small house behind the hospital with George Eberle, who had moved over to Thimphu the day before. We were able to continue playing chess, for which we had developed a passion, as a way of passing the cold winter evenings. We visited Dr. Tobgyel, the King's personal physician, at his office in the dzong; a quiet and courteous man bearing a serious responsibility as medical adviser to the King, he told us that an audience with His Majesty was arranged for the following morning.

Dressed in our best suits, George Eberle and I reported to Dr. Tobgyel's office at the appointed hour of 9 a.m. Half an hour later a message came to say that His Majesty was moving up the valley to his palace at Dechen Chholing because of the noise of workmen in the dzong. The King travelled in an open army car with a jeep load of the Royal Bodyguard before and behind, red lights flashing and sirens wailing. Labourers stopped working to bow in homage as he was driven sedately up the road. The royal standard, bearing a golden dragon against a yellow and cerise background, was lowered from a pole outside the dzong indicating that the King was no longer in residence. Drukpa means "People of the Land of the Thunder Dragon" and refers to the pure Bhutanese.

We followed in Dr. Tobgyel's jeep, maintaining a discreet distance. The royal palace stands on a hill surrounded by grounds laid out by the King himself, which slope down to the river. Entering by a side gate we were led into a courtyard where members of the Royal Bodyguard were practising a ceremonial dance.

Fifty large and handsome men – qualities essential for their selection to this corps d'elite of the Bhutanese Army – formed a circle and were gyrating slowly, their hands and arms performing expressive and symbolic gestures accompanying a mournful song. Wearing dark blue boku with maroon berets, they are smart, highly-trained soldiers similar to our own Household Cavalry.

Inside the palace the King has his own servants; to be one is a prized honour and is an apprenticeship for government service. If a young man shows intelligence and promise he may be selected as a servant of the King, thus he can be evaluated and placed in an appropriate junior position in the government. Many of the thrimpons we met had started their careers in this manner.

George Eberle and I were shown into an upper room where we waited for ten minutes. On the floor lay skins of leopard, tiger and black panther, shot by the King on his hunting expeditions. In front of us stood small carved tables, vividly painted. We sat on low couches draped with Bhutanese cloth woven with many gaudy colours, especially crimson and gold.

Moments of intense activity with servants scurrying to and fro preceded the entry of the King. I formally presented to him my gifts, a book on rifles and some gun oil from Cogswell and Harrison of St. James's, and an ashi kadar – a genuine white silk scarf I had bought in Darjeeling. The presents were handed to Dr. Tobgyel, as by custom they are not inspected immediately. A pleasant and relaxed hour was spent discussing George Eberle's yak disease and my goitre project. The King has a thorough knowledge of every region of his country, having travelled from the northern mountains to the southern jungles, throughout the west and the east. He enlarged on many details of our proposed route to the east and, most valuable of all, gave me unqualified encouragement about taking our children. During the previous days I had met a number of people with whom I discussed our plans; each signified horror that I should be contemplating a journey across the high passes of central Bhutan in the middle of winter with my family and gloomily described snowbound passes and the bitter cold in an attempt to dissuade me. I was beginning to feel disheartened, wondering if we had not taken on something too big for us; but the King was disarmingly frank about the problems we might encounter and made it clear that he considered it to be a splendid adventure, so my flagging confidence was boosted. He had taken his own children on journeys and saw no reason why we should not do likewise. He remembered much of our conversation at the Dorchester Hotel four years before and told me that he had kept the photograph of Sarah and

Adam, on the back of which I had written our address. In the background of the picture was our pink thatched cottage in Suffolk, and we laughed again over the description of it by one of our Nepali Tamang boys "Kulli ko ghar josto" – just like a coolie's house and not expected for a doctor sahib.

At the end of an hour the King excused himself for ending the audience as he had some government ministers waiting to see him. We bowed and made our exit. Outside on the landing stood a number of high ranking officials who had been waiting patiently for a considerable time. One of the Royal Bodyguard, jumping to action as we left, inadvertently kicked me on the ankle making me wince with pain.

Later in the day I went to the dzong to meet the King's half-brother, Dasho Namgyal Wangchuk, the Paro Penlop, whose mother, Ashi Pema Dechen, we had met in Calcutta. He was twenty-eight years old and spoke perfect English, having been educated in Darjeeling. He discussed with astute foresight the problems of Bhutan's precipitate advance into the twentieth century and of their political relationships with surrounding countries, by whom Bhutan is landlocked. We talked of our journey and he reiterated the King's opinion that we would be able to take the children with no harm as he had travelled much of our route on tour the previous November. He placed absolutely no restrictions on our movements in Bhutan and generously offered us the use of his house in Bumthang.

I must now make a digression in order to explain the history of Bhutan that has led to the present dynasty.

In the eighth century A.D. Bhutan was ruled by many independent princes, the most powerful called Sindu Raja, who was converted to Buddhism by Padma Sambhava, an Indian saint. It is not clear how much fact is behind the story of the tiger flying to Taktsang with the lama on his back bringing Buddhism to Bhutan. During the next seven centuries various Tibetan kings crossed the Himalayas to ravage Bhutan's green valleys, which offered comfort from the unceasing wind and bleakness of their plateau homeland.

In A.D. 1557 Dujom Dorji, a powerful lama from Ralung, the

famous Drukpa monastery and original headquarters of the Red-hat sect of lamas, repulsed repeated invasions from Tibet and became master of the whole country, taking the title of Dharma Raja – the first of a line that extended across the next four centuries. During his reign the building of all the big dzongs was started. The Dharma Raja was the spiritual head of the country and "that he might wholly devote himself to the interests of religion he appointed a regent for temporal affairs called the Deb Raja" (Wessels).

Two Portuguese Jesuit Fathers, Cacella and Cabral, set out from Bengal in 1627 to enter Bhutan with the intention of proceeding to Tibet. They were perhaps the first Europeans to penetrate into this mountainous region and their letters gave the first accurate report of Bhutan and its people to the Western world. Their journey was perilous and they were twice robbed and imprisoned before meeting the King. The latter must have been the second Dharma Raja, successor to Dujom Dorji, at once King and grand lama of Cambirasi or Mon, an area including north-eastern Bhutan up to Phari and as far as Gyantse in Tibet. The King's home in peaceful times was at Ralung near Gyantse, but when the Jesuits met him he was touring the mountains of Bhutan maintaining order and quelling uprisings by the kingdoms in the east of the country. Cacella and Cabral spent three months travelling with the King, who was offended when they suggested leaving to go to Tibet to join another priest called Andrade, then at Tsaparang. To encourage the Jesuits to stay, the King, a scholar who enjoyed the company of other intellectuals, gave them leave to preach Christianity and promised to build them a house and a church at Paro. But the priests' wishes prevailed and they left Bhutan to visit the King of U-Tsang at Shigatse, where Cacella died in 1630. Cabral crossed the Himalayas into Nepal and continued a life of adventure.

For more than a hundred years nothing is heard about Bhutan until 1772 when the Deb Judhur laid claim to Cooch Behar, swept down on it from the hills and carried off the Raja. The East India Company controlled British interests in India and Warren Hastings, the Governor-General, sent Captain Jones with a force of troops to suppress the Bhutanese. Jones captured

Dalimkotta Duar but died of malaria, prevalent to this day in the dense, tiger-infested jungle bordering the Himalayan foothills, known as the Terai in Nepal and the Duars, or Dooars, in Bengal and Assam. This narrow strip of land south of Bhutan, ten to twenty miles wide and 250 miles long, is entered by eighteen passes (or doors) from the hills; eleven are adjacent to Bhutan, seven in Assam.

The Deb Judhur had made himself unpopular at home as Tassisudon (Tashichho Dzong) had been burnt down and he tried to rebuild it in one year using forced labour. While he was out of the country at Buxa Duar fighting Captain Jones, a lama's party tried to take over the government and on his return the Deb was compelled to take refuge in Simtokha Dzong twelve miles below Tashichho Dzong.

The Bhutanese asked the Tashi (or Teshoo) Lama, Panchen Rimpoche, to intervene in their favour as mediator with the East India Company. The Tashi Lama was then the Regent of Tibet and guardian of the Dalai Lama, not yet of age. He was described as a man "venerated on account of his sacred office and not less beloved for the benevolence of his character and the courtesy of his manners". His letter to Warren Hastings is a striking example of oriental diplomacy carrying a threat shrouded in meek and suppliant terms.

Warren Hastings commissioned Mr. George Bogle in 1774 as emissary of the Company to make a treaty of peace with Bhutan and to negotiate opening a trade route to Tibet. As present-day Sikkim was then part of Nepal, whose doors were closed to the world, the easy route north to Tibet by the Natu La into the Chumbi Valley was not accessible.

Bogle set out in company with Dr. Hamilton carrying a large supply of potatoes which they were ordered by Warren Hastings to plant at each halting place – the first introduction of the plant now grown throughout Bhutan. Bogle had friendly discussions with the Deb Raja and reported them to the Governor-General: Europeans would not be allowed to travel in Bhutan although Hindu and Muslim merchants might do so; the Deb was given permission for Bhutanese to attend an annual trade fair at Rangpur in the plains and to visit Calcutta to trade; Bogle tried to arrange for a trade centre in Bhutan midway between Tibet and Bengal.

Bogle was detained in Bhutan as passports for entry to Tibet were refused by the Tashi Lama on the pretence of an order from the Chinese Emperor, whose sovereignty he acknowledged. But the Tashi Lama must have recanted and Bogle travelled by Phari to Tashilumpo to meet him and they became such good friends that Bogle was entrusted with money to build a temple on the banks of the Ganges. The two men arranged to meet in Peking at a later date but the Tashi Lama died of smallpox on arrival there in 1781, the same year as Bogle died in Calcutta.

Dr. Hamilton then led two missions to Bhutan; the first in 1775 to examine a border dispute which he decided in favour of Bhutan, the second two years after, to congratulate the Deb Raja on his succession.

In 1783 Captain Samuel Turner was sent to Tibet by Warren Hastings in company with Dr. Saunders and Lt. Davis to congratulate the reincarnation of the Tashi Lama and to confirm friendly relations with Tibet. He spent some time wandering through Bhutan and writing detailed observations on his journey. He was caught up in a rebellion when the Deb Raja's troops, using bows and arrows, blockaded and captured Wangdu Phodrang whose governor (called the zimpon, the same as dzongpen and thrimpon) was leading the insurrection. On the advice of Dr. Hamilton, Turner tactfully ceded two disputed border territories to Bhutan and left for Tibet after a stay of three months.

Again a period of silence reigns over the history of Bhutan lasting more than fifty years, during which the Nepalese invaded Tibet (1792) but were driven back and soundly defeated in a battle only twenty miles from Kathmandu. After this war all passes of Tibet were closed to natives of India and they have remained shut with few exceptions ever since.

In 1838 Captain Pemberton with Dr. Griffith and twenty-five Assam police crossed Bhutan from east to west, finding the country "in a state of continual anarchy . . . and incessant struggles between the Tongsa Penlop and the Paro Penlop". As well as fighting internecine wars the Bhutanese were constantly aggressive along the Indian frontier and many incidents occurred, leading to Ashley Eden's mission in 1864. Eden met constant obstacles and interruptions and the Bhutan Assembly, "with audacious insolence", compelled him to sign the restitution of the Assam Duars and enforced their demands by stopping supplies to his missions and even committing personal outrages.

To punish the Bhutanese for their ill-treatment of Eden's mission, Britain declared war, annexed the Duars and demanded compensation of 50,000 rupees annually. After a battle at Dewangiri some guns and prisoners fell into the hands of the Tongsa Penlop and two British soldiers are said to have been kept in Tongsa Dzong for a short period. The Bhutan-Duars war took place in 1865 and twenty years later the last civil war in Bhutan was fought. Jigme Namgyal, the Tongsa Penlop, joined forces with the Paro Penlop to quash an uprising of the Thimphu and Punakha dzongpens.

In 1897 an earthquake destroyed Punakha Dzong and with it went much of the recorded history of Bhutan. From the turn of the twentieth century Bhutan entered a new phase of her history when her contacts with the outside world became more tangible and personal. The Tongsa Penlop, Ugyen Wangchuk, accompanied the 1904 Younghusband Expedition to Lhasa as a mediator and in return for his services was awarded the order of Knight Commander of the Indian Empire. John Claude White travelled to Bhutan to present the order on behalf of King Edward VII of England. Two years later, in 1907, White again went to Bhutan, with a caravan of two hundred and sixty-four loads, to attend the installation of Ugyen Wangchuk as Gyelpo or King, which came about in the following way. The Dharma Raja had died and as no incarnation was found the Deb held both offices, but he was a recluse following a spiritual life, and consequently power fell into the hands of the strong man of the country – the Tongsa Penlop. Lamas, officials and laymen unanimously voted to abolish the four hundred year old offices of Deb and Dharma Raja, proclaimed Ugyen Wangchuk the first Gyelpo and declared the title hereditary.

Britain signed a treaty in 1910 pledging herself not to interfere with the internal administration of Bhutan, who agreed in turn to be guided by the advice of Britain in their external relations. The Gyelpo visited Delhi for the Durbar of King George V the next year and frequent visits to India, and indeed all over the world, have become the custom of Bhutanese royalty.

Sir Ugyen Wangchuk died in 1926 and was succeeded by Jigme Wangchuk, who married two sisters, both still alive, Ashi Choden and Ashi Pema Dechen. Ashi Choden had one son, Jigme Dorji Wangchuk. Bhutan's doors during this time remained tight shut to the outside world and few foreigners entered the country. Lord Ronaldshay, the Governor of Bengal, went to present the K.C.I.E. to the King in 1921. A botanist named Bailey travelled in West and Central Bhutan in 1924 and found the rare blue Himalayan poppy *Meconopsis Betonicifolia*. Two more botanists, Sherriff and Ludlow, made extensive journeys into every quarter of Bhutan; in 1933 they crossed from west to east, in 1934 and 1936 they collected plants in the east and crossed into Tibet and in 1938 they were again in the east with Taylor, prior to going north to explore the gorges of the Tsangpo in Tibet. They made two plant collecting expeditions soon after the war mainly in East Bhutan. Sherriff and Ludlow knew Bhutan as no foreigner had ever done before.

In 1952 Jigme Dorji Wangchuk was made Gyelpo of Bhutan. His wife Ashi Kesang is the daughter of the late Sonam Tobgyal Dorji, who had been Deb Zimpon under the King's father, and whose son Jigme Dorji succeeded him as prime minister. Since the assassination of Jigme Dorji in 1964 the King now rules the country with the help of the National Assembly.

I travelled down to Phuntsoling several days later to meet my family, Sarah having cabled to say she would arrive on the Kalimpong bus. We spent a hectic morning in the bazaar shopping for the next four months as food was cheaper than at Thimphu and the selection much greater. I bought eight light, cheap tin trunks, intending they should be disposable. We bought a selection of essentials, porridge, powdered milk, sugar, dehydrated peas; and a few luxuries – jam, sweets and chutney. Our problem was to keep our weight to a minimum and I estimated we would have about twelve sixty-pound loads, allowing six loads of food, two of medical equipment, two of clothing and bedding, one of cooking utensils and one of tents. Dr. Roy, the medical officer in Phuntsoling, advised us on the best shops and supplied me with medicines from the government storerooms for use in clinics.

The following day we piled our mountain of equipment into a jeep, crammed Lakpa Doma on top, heavily dosed against car sickness, held the children on our knees and set off for Thimphu. The eight-hour journey was uncomfortable and we were relieved to arrive safely before nightfall.

The following day was a national holiday for the King's birthday. An important archery match took place, where we met two English girls, the only British people resident in Bhutan, (fewer than ten Europeans live in the whole country). Rowena Pratt had been governess to the royal children for eighteen months and was starting a school in the Bhutanese military camp at the request of the Paro Penlop; Caroline, her sister, was teaching in the government high school. The girls had been brought up on a farm on the side of Cader Idris in wildest mid-Wales, so were accustomed to the rigours and privations of their life in Bhutan, but they were especially glad of Sarah's company, and gave us much interesting background knowledge.

Dr. Sandup, the doctor in charge of the Thimphu hospital, told us he had been ordered to allocate one of his trainee compounders to accompany us on our journey as interpreter and assistant. He said we must be strict with the boy, who was prone to dreaming. Later Chhimi Wangchuk presented himself at our house; he was about eighteen years old, powerfully built with legs like tree trunks and a bullet head with close-cropped black hair. He had evidently put on his best boku fo this occasion but his shirt sleeves had not been washed recently. At first he was nervous and reticent but pleased with his assignment that would take him away from the routine in the hospital for a few months. Chhimi's father was the thrimpon of Wangdu Phodrang Dzong and his uncle the thrimpon in Bumthang. He spoke both the dialect of his native Bumthang, and Dzonka, the official national tongue spoken in the west. Further to the east around

Tashigang, yet another totally different language, Shashup, is spoken.

Chhimi's English was poor; I needed to speak slowly at first with some explanations in Nepali but he learnt fast. I explained to him the entire plan of our journey across Bhutan and as much about the medical work as he could understand. He set to work with vigour packing food and equipment into the tin trunks and making them up into sixty-pound loads, which he parcelled in sacking and tied securely with rope. To his credit they remained unharmed after many weeks of travelling despite much rough handling. My trunks with the blood sampling equipment had arrived from Calcutta after much delay. In the hospital and the leprosarium further down the valley we collected some blood samples to send off to Dr. Mourant as a preliminary test of our scheme for transportation. We first cooled the blood tubes in the river and then despatched them in a tin, requesting a cabled report on their condition after arrival. Adam was excited by these preparations and busied himself helping the men: he idolised Chhimi and followed him, copying every movement; Judith was closely attached to Lakpa Doma, so between them the children had formed two firm friendships that remained throughout the succeeding months.

The week of preparations passed quickly. Besides sorting food and preparing clothes, Sarah made a visit to Paro. The altitude of Thimphu was 8,100 feet and the night temperature was well below freezing; we breakfasted in the warm morning sunshine. When the noon wind rose we retired to our house to play chess or sleep until it ceased blowing in late afternoon. In the evening we sauntered among the stalls and shops of the bazaar, enthralled by the intense activity. But we were anxious to get on with our journey.

Wangdu Phodrang Bridge

## CHAPTER 8

On February 18th, 1967, we left Thimphu on our journey east-wards across Bhutan. The hospital ambulance, lent to us for the first part of the road to Wangdu Phodrang, was loaded to the roof with trunks securely tied in sacking. The morning was over-cast but we all felt happy to be on our way with our problems of the past weeks behind us.

The road turned east at Simtokha Dzong and climbed steadily through pine forest towards the Dochu La. A dusting of snow lay on the hilltops and small heaps remained by the roadside in ditches and under leeward banks. After two hours we arrived at the pass at 10,400 feet and were surrounded by swirling mist, which denied us any view of the mountains usually well seen from here. Recent days in Thimphu had been clear so we were sad not to have even a glimpse of the country in store for us. The disappointment of reaching longed-for vistas and finding them obscured is intense because there is often neither time to dwell nor opportunity to return. But the reward is ample when wide horizons are visible, making previous disappointments fade into oblivion.

We drank a cup of hot tea and ate some cakes in a Tibetan tea-house standing beside a long mani wall on the summit of the Dochu La. The driver and Chhimi began a snowball fight so Adam and I joined in, to the delight and amazement of the onlooking travellers. The exercise warmed us and created a welcome diversion from the cramped vehicle.

Our road descended through dense jungle. Adam sat on Chhimi's lap on the tailboard while Judith slept on Sarah's knee. She occasionally woke and tried to change gear for the driver which was alarming on the precipitous bends. Both children were good travellers and caused us no worry with sickness or boredom.

Many features of interest on the descent made up for our lack of views. We passed some rhododendron trees in full bloom, their vivid splash of colour breaking the monotony of the dark green trees; lower down some white magnolia flowers, a gentle pink when their bud was closed, contrasted with a flaming scarlet blossom growing on an awkward, ungraceful tree. The season was early for flowers but these foretold the glory of this forest a few months hence.

Beyond the trees where the valley opened, the hillsides had a parched, pre-monsoon appearance. Slopes that had been ploughed prior to planting were predominantly ochre and sepia in colour; the river bed showed gentle greys and blues. After the rains rice and grass spring up and a green luxuriance takes the place of sombre pastel shades. Passing damp culverts, which channelled only a trickling stream, we saw an abundance of deep purple primulae growing in rocky crevices. A long stalked multiheaded primula, somewhat paler in colour, grew in the less shaded areas on the open hillside.

We stopped to collect some rhododendron flowers, Chhimi, with great agility, shinning up the tree whose outer branches overhung a deep chasm. His ape-like performance ecstatically amused Adam, who had to be restrained from following his new-found hero. Appropriately, round the next corner we encountered a colony of tame white monkeys the size of baboons who entertained us with gymnastic feats on the rocks. In the distant woods we heard barking deer, small fawn coloured animals with no horns.

After midday we reached the end of the road at a small village called Lometsawa. As we waved farewell to the jeep on its return to Thimphu, we realised that from here till Tashigang, nearly two hundred miles away on the other side of the country, we would see no roads or vehicles; at last our real journey had begun. Chhimi's friend, who had accompanied us to help with unloading, looked sad and deeply envious of the freedom and adventures in store for us during the months ahead; he was a particularly good boy and we would have liked him to accompany us but this could not be.

Chhimi approached the Tibetan owner of the shack at the roadhead.

"Where are the ponies that were ordered from Thimphu?"

"What ponies?" he replied. "I've no ponies, they're all up the hill grazing."

"But Wangdu Phodrang Thrimpon ordered ponies," Chhimi insisted. "I know, because he's my father."

"Oh!" said the Tibetan, as if this fact made some difference, "We'll have to see what can be done."

On this and on many similar occasions when transport that had been ordered in advance failed to arrive, I determined not to get angry or emotionally involved. Sarah, the children and I retired to the shack leaving Chhimi to solve the problem, which he did in masterly fashion. All his diffidence and shyness of the first few days had vanished; he took pride in his assignment as our aide-de-camp and exerted his authority with such confidence that shortly four scrawny ponies arrived; enough to start with. Chhimi generously volunteered to return in the evening to bring the remainder of the luggage. A large plate of noodles from a steaming cauldron on the open hearth filled our empty stomachs; the children showed no surprise at being in the world of shabby inns and tea-houses.

Sarah was teaching Lakpa the precautions she determined to follow in order to avoid stomach troubles. She insisted on boiling all drinking water; as we drank nothing but well stewed tea this created no problem – Judith's first spoken word after learning the traditional parental greetings was "char". On the rare occasions when we acquired meat we boiled or fried it well. As supplies in the centre of Bhutan were reported to be scarce our family's impartiality to all kinds of food was a real asset. We were hoping as far as possible to live off the land for our basic foods, so we could not afford to be choosy over what we ate. Adam has always been a voracious eater, quite unselective provided the quantity was adequate – a true son of his father in this and many other respects.

Outside, Chhimi was arguing vociferously with the Tibetan hotelier. He then came in to report that he had settled the fee for the horses and had arranged that the same man would return for the remaining loads that evening and bring them early the next day – when, and not before, he would be paid.

The first day's manner of travelling was experimental and needed to be modified subsequently. We wanted to reach Wangdu Phodrang before nightfall so we decided the children should ride two ponies, our essential luggage coming on the other two beasts. Two bedding rolls were lashed longways to the rough wooden pack saddle. Such rolls have been a traditional item of travelling equipment in India since the days of the Imperial Raj; made of strong canvas, they are laid out flat on the ground and blankets or sleeping bags, clothes and personal gear are rolled up tightly and secured with leather straps. When fully packed the roll measured three feet long by two feet wide, and we found it a useful and practical method of storing soft luggage. The children were seated on a cushion of foam rubber laid across the saddle between the rolls.

The wind had now risen, blowing sand in gusts and whistling through the stunted bushes leading down towards the river bank. Adam set off on his own mount, Sarah and Lakpa walking beside him; round his face he wrapped his Nepali blanket, an inseparable favourite since cradle days, to keep off the biting headwind. I stayed behind with Judith to supervise the loading of the two pack ponies that Chhimi was to escort; she wandered off alone and we found her playing with some bristly pigs eating swill from a trough and responding to her friendly advances with coarse grunts. I tied a strap round Judith for safety, keeping hold of one end, and we set off down a steep bank; I was reminded of the terror I had felt standing at the top of such a descent while skiing the Haute Route in the Alps the previous year. She appeared unperturbed so long as I was close beside to steady her with my hand when the path became rough.

In a narrow place beside the river I had a fright and was persuaded we would need to alter radically the method of saddling for the children. A caravan of mules approaching from the opposite direction forced me to drop behind Judith because the path was only wide enough for two animals to pass. The muleteer whacked his mules from behind to speed them up, they took fright, mounted the bank and pushed us to the outside edge, where there was a drop of fifty feet into the foaming torrent. Judith's pony shied, cantered forwards, and I was just able to catch her before she was thrown off. She was quite unmoved by this experience but I took several minutes to recover, my legs felt like lead and my heart was palpitating wildly. Sarah was well ahead and did not witness this narrow escape. Judith was too small to ride by herself and I decided that she would sit on a pony with Sarah in future, while Chhimi and I would walk beside Adam.

Darkness had nearly fallen when we reached the bridge and we climbed towards the lights of the dzong shining high above us. Wangdu Phodrang bridge is built on an island of shingle, and in the middle of the river like a miniature castle is a bulwark of stones, whence spring the five cantilevers supporting the main part of the bridge that spans the wide river at its deepest point as it swings towards the bank. Single joisted beams bridge the shorter space between the island and the far bank. Three gate house turrets gave a beauty and dignity to this unique structure.

Chhimi had raced ahead to announce our arrival and make ready the guest house beside the dzong where we were to stay. On reaching the house Sarah and Lakpa climbed some dark stairs to an upper room and prepared the children for bed. They needed warm pullovers besides their Terylene sleeping bags. We had long since stopped changing them into pyjamas; they merely had a complete change of clothes on the infrequent occasions when they bathed. We considered following the

Suffolk custom of basting them with pig's grease and sewing them into their underclothes from Michaelmas until May.

Our daily routine consisted of washing faces and hands, brushing teeth and attending to our arthropod infestations; Judith and Sarah already had head lice, so Lakpa plucked out the elusive creatures and bit them between her teeth making a popping sound; then she combed their hair for eggs and finally washed it. No social stigma was attached to this performance, even on a doctor's wife and child. It reminded me of an occasion when I was in the pet "zoo" of a large London store watching two monkeys similarly occupied. A Knightsbridge lady turned to me and exclaimed in a haughty voice, "But surely, there are no fleas on a Harrods monkey!"

Adam and I never had lice but we suffered badly from fleas, which crawled round our midriff, biting as they went and leaving irritating spots in their wake. I was unable to explain this sex preference of our parasites. Into our clothing and sleeping bags we liberally sprinkled D.D.T. powder and this helped to keep the enemy at bay.

Chhimi and I retired to the cooking shed attached to the guest house, built up a good fire and decided we would surprise the women by cooking supper. We measured out the rice in a large mug and threw it into a metal pot of boiling water; the rice swelled in volume and overspilled the top. When we realised we had selected the wrong sized mug we collapsed on the floor in uncontrolled mirth which the women, having just arrived, found hard to understand. That evening as we tucked into a mountain of boiled rice we laughed at anything and everything, maybe because of our new found freedom, maybe because of the mild hysteria of setting off into the wilds with all its attendant uncertainties.

The following morning Chhimi and I had an appointment in the dzong to meet Dasho Thrimpon, his father. In Thimphu I had bought a dark green boku as Chhimi insisted that wearing Bhutanese clothes in the dzongs would be appreciated. He dressed me with care making sure that my boku was the correct height above the knee, that my cuffs were showing the correct length and most important, that my kabngy, the white dzong scarf, was wound round my shoulder according to fashion. I found difficulty in maintaining it in place as it tended to slip off. The much rehearsed performance of bowing and holding one end forwards in formal greeting filled me with alarm. Chhimi showed concern that my etiquette and attire should be faultless, in the manner of a child being visited by his parents at boarding school and terrified by the critical gaze of his fellows.

In front of the dzong steps stood a mighty prayer flag against which a man was doing a headstand as punishment for being in the dzong without his kabngy. From the painted courtyard we climbed a wide flight of stairs to an upper apartment. Chhimi showed me into a room where the thrimpon was seated on a low couch. He rose and we exchanged greetings; I presented him with a pictorial calendar, several of which we had brought from home for such occasions. With Chhimi interpreting, we had a friendly discourse on the merits of thatched roofs, large red buses and English policemen. The calendar proved an invaluable talking point and caused my host much amusement. From where I sat by the unglazed window I could see our children outside playing in the sunshine. Butter tea and chura, a crisp fried rice, were served to us by the thrimpon's wife, while Chhimi stood beside his father in respectful attendance. The thrimpon had accompanied Ludlow and Sherriff on their botanical expeditions in the nineteen thirties and when he was a boy he had met Bailey. At the conclusion of the interview, eggs, rice and onions were presented to me, then we took our leave.

I walked round the walls of the dzong, which is built on a tongue of land high above the confluence of the Punakha (Mo) Chhu and the Tang Chhu. From such a height it commands a view over the bridge and the main road, which climbs the cliffside from the river. The defensibility of this fortress is assured by the sheer walls of the promontory falling five hundred feet on three sides. Wangdu Phodrang's reputation for being the windiest place in Bhutan was justified by the gale and dust storm that raged all the afternoon so that even the Tibetans, whose stalls and booths filled the bazaar, retired to shelter.

An air of excitement pervaded our camp that evening as we discussed our final preparations for moving off next day on the first leg of the journey to Tongsa, which we thought would take about one week. Chhimi spent much of the day in the dzong organising ponies. The whole business of travel arrangements proved remarkably simple: throughout Bhutan government standards exist; one load weighs sixty pounds, the fixed price being five rupees per day; a pack pony carries two sixty-pound loads, costing double; a riding pony costs fifteen rupees per day. No argument or bargaining over these rates is possible, and furthermore on all the main routes across the country government stages are fixed. If a five-day journey is completed in four days the men are still entitled to a full five days' payment. This avoided the unpleasant haggling inevitable in the freelance system in Nepal where travellers are at the mercy of sit-down strikes by their coolies, against whom they have no redress despite thumb-print stamped "contracts". In Bhutan a government officer or traveller needing porters or ponies must notify the thrimpon in advance of the day he intends to leave and the number of loads. The thrimpon keeps a rota of villages in his region, which are obliged in turn to supply government labour for a fixed wage, be it for bridge building, road maintenance or any other community labour. The thrimpon sends the messenger of the "duty" village, who is temporarily resident in the dzong, to his headman. The latter has a list of families in the village who supply labour in rotation and the head of the family is notified of the time and place the services are required. The family must then decide who should go. This authoritarian system has much to commend it for efficiency and fairness in the division of labour and is no less democratic than was our own obligatory national service.

Lakpa started by sleeping in our room at Kalimpong and, during the entire journey in Bhutan, she never left the foot of our bed because she was so afraid of Bhutanese men. She was a very pretty girl with a charming face and bright smile whom the men were quick to notice; they paid her much attention but received no encouragement. She had a placid nature but was unusually out of sorts that evening.

"I will flatter her," said Chhimi after a few moments' thought.

"It's kindness she needs, not flattery," Sarah replied. Chhimi's attitude was characteristic of the rough way Bhutanese men treat

84

their women, a factor contributing to the hardness of their looks; by comparison Lakpa must have appeared very attractive.

From then on Chhimi took good care of Lakpa and Sarah, being as reliable and faithful as he was generous. Together we discussed the question of taking a cook but decided it was easier for Sarah and Lakpa to manage on their own, especially regarding the children's food. By keeping the party small we gained a greater independence. Also we intended to eat all together, a habit which at first caused concern to the people but they soon became used to such a strangely democratic notion.

Tongsa Dzong
Family caravan

Charungkashor Stupa

## CHAPTER 9

Next morning, before we were up, we heard the noise of ponies being marshalled outside the guest house and the chatter of men's voices. The ponies arrived in ones and twos. Disorganisation was the rule on all first days before a routine had been established. A young police officer added a voice of authority to Chhimi's protestations; we quietly breakfasted leaving him to get on with his harangue. Adam was excited and ran around helping Chhimi. Six pack ponies were despatched and by 10 a.m. we were ready to depart.

Sarah folded one of our foam rubber mattresses over her saddle for comfort, which also allowed room for Judith to sit on the pommel in front of her. We tied Judith's christening blanket round her tummy and behind Sarah's back; this supported her when she fell asleep, making less burden for Sarah. Judith's dummy, one of a dozen brought from home, was firmly tied round her neck on a piece of string. Lakpa mounted a pony and was insecure for several days until she got used to riding.

We altered Adam's saddling after the alarming experiences of Judith's short ride from Lometsawa. Two bedding rolls were placed longways as before; a foam cushion was lashed firmly over the wooden saddle with webbing straps; behind this a rolled mattress was placed forming a back rest, so that Adam sat as if in a large armchair with his feet straight ahead beside the pony's neck. We tied a dzong scarf loosely round his middle, allowing plenty of room to lift him free; the six foot long ends of the scarf were tucked under the forward straps of the bedding roll, taken under the rear straps, then tied back into his waistband. This harness was firmly anchored but allowed Adam to be extricated without unfastening the whole thing. He could hold on to the front arms of the scarf like a pair of reins, which gave him a feeling of support. Aloysius, Adam's teddy bear, rode beside him with his legs tucked into the harness. Chhimi and I agreed that one or other of us must always walk with Adam's horse in case difficulties arose. This manner of travelling proved satisfactory from the first and only minor adjustments were necessary.

From Wangdu Phodrang we could see our path cutting horizontally across a mountain in the middle distance and leading far into the Tang Chhu Valley. As we set off and looked back at the thrimpon and the dzong workers waving to us, we felt like a bottle of champagne whose cork had popped.

The first three hours on our path proved an exciting introduction. After an early steep climb the new bazaar of Wangdu Phodrang, replacing that burnt down the previous year, lay several hundred feet below us by the banks of the river. The ponies' partiality for walking on the extreme outside edge of the narrow path caused me some alarm, as Adam, though himself quite unconcerned, appeared to be hanging in space. The ponies intuitively do this in order to avoid catching their inside load on the bank, so throwing them off balance. I soon came to trust their surefootedness, reliability and strength despite their lean and hungry appearance. The best of them are of the Tangun breed, indigenous to Tibet.

Rounding a corner only an hour after we set off, a deafening roar came from an army firing range in the valley. The front ponies shied and turned to escape. Adam's pony was buffeted by the one ahead and, trying to turn in the narrow space of the path where it was cutting into a culvert, reversed over the bank, which gave way and began to break up under the slithering hooves of the frightened animal. Adam was thrown backwards but was held in place by his waist band.

"Hold tight!" I shouted. "Don't let go of your scarf whatever happens." The pony stood with his front hooves on the path and his back ones three feet down the precipitous and crumbling bank. Chhimi ran back when he heard me shout and quietened the beast by talking gently to it and supporting the slipping loads. We lifted Adam out of his harness and then righted the pony. I was far more frightened than my son, who was quite unaware of the danger in his position. Chhimi has a thorough knowledge of horses, having spent much of his boyhood grazing ponies up on the high pastures of his native Bumthang. He had been apprenticed to a lama but, finding the discipline intolerable, ran away and went to school at the age of eleven on the insistence of his wise uncle, now the thrimpon of Byakar Dzong.

I ran down into the valley to ask the officer in charge to stop firing while we let the ponies pass. He was reluctant until I mentioned the Paro Penlop, his commander-in-chief, whose name immediately gained his acquiescence. After this interruption Adam continued singing his nursery rhymes where he had left off and began to sway in gentle rhythm with the movements of the pony; I stayed close beside him.

Our caravan settled down to an orderly pace and we passed through rhododendron woods but only a few trees were in bloom. One strangely leafless tree grew a flower the shape and colour of a water lily. We halted for lunch by a stream at Chhudzomsa (the water meeting place), where flies were thick and obnoxious, causing Judith much annoyance. As we climbed after lunch leaving behind the humid valley floor, the flies became less of a nuisance. The steepest parts of the road were cut out of the hillside like a ladder of steps, which the ponies took at a trot to gather momentum; it was hard work trying to run beside Adam and lend a supporting hand against his back; he clung on firmly and soon got the idea of leaning forward over the horse's neck when going up and leaning backwards on the descent. Sarah, having ridden since childhood, is a competent horsewoman so had no problem even with Judith balanced on the saddle in front of her. Lakpa looked the least secure of the whole caravan.

We continued to climb for another three hours and were tired when we reached Samtengang (6,700 feet) in the late afternoon. The school was vacant so we occupied the verandah and made ourselves at home in a small cook house. The children were pleased to be on firm ground again and wandered off to collect firewood. Adam decided he would join the ponymen and squatted round their fire telling them long and involved stories of his flight to India by jet aeroplane, accompanied by the appropriate sounds and gestures. They were very amused although they understood nothing of what he said.

Next morning our departure was more orderly, each man knowing exactly which load belonged to him. We were on the road by 7.30 a.m., having eaten a good breakfast of the eggs Chhimi's father had given us. A large bowl of porridge washed down with sweet tea lined our stomachs, now well attuned to the change in diet. The children had no special fads and ate anything. Chhimi made it his job to hunt out and buy any food he could find from habitations we passed on our way; he became an expert forager so we rarely went short of eggs and milk, so fundamental to our diet.

From Samtengang we soon came on the crest of a ridge between two rivers passing through tall pine trees with soft needles lying underfoot. Patches of sunlight appearing below heavy cumulus lit up distant wheatfields against the sombre green surroundings. The path took to the south side of the hill rising gradually through stunted oak trees and holly bushes; cresting Tshasabolu (9,320 feet) we stopped for the lunch halt just before midday. This high open pasture gave us an expansive feeling and wide views of distant mountains.

The 2,500 feet descent to the Tang Chhu was mostly too steep to ride. Adam and I played at being aeroplanes, holding our arms sideways as wings and running down the hill, occasionally tumbling into piles of dead leaves. Judith walked and ran between Sarah and Lakpa. Considering the difficulty I used to have in encouraging any member of the family to walk as far as the corner shop back in Cambridge, I was pleasantly surprised by the way they managed this long and tiring descent and how little they were worried by the steep exposure. Dismounting at places on the path unsuitable for riding helped to relieve the monotony of long hours in the saddle.

Dark clouds accumulated during the late afternoon and rain began to fall as we crossed Radzao Bridge. We looked for a cave or some other shelter but nothing suitable could be found. Adam, no longer able to contain his tiredness after the long day, fell asleep in his saddle; he was safe enough on the flat valley floor, rolling with the motion of the pony. I tried to curl him up and rest his lolling head on one of the bedding rolls, to prevent it jerking backwards.

We chose a beautiful camp site beside the river in a small opening among the bushes; I expected a drenching so we put up the tent for Sarah, Lakpa and the children. It was a high altitude model with a flysheet over an outer frame, very light and easy to assemble, designed for the American Everest Expedition. Chhimi and I arranged a bivouac between the loads under a covering of plastic sheeting.

That night our bedtime story had a touch of magic about it; we sat round a fire of huge logs together with the ponymen, who looked sinister huddled under their cloaks; in the darkness behind their shoulders the ponies munched grass and the river played its gentle melody. By the light of the fire we read a story which was as much appreciated by the ponymen as the children. We had brought a number of the children's own books and toys so they would not feel too far removed from home and their own possessions. After the story Lakpa took the children off to bed and sang to Judith, patting her back until she went to sleep.

The next day was clear, the storm having passed. We climbed to Rithang through woods where mauve and white azalea bushes with a fragrant smell were growing. To the north a magnificent view of the headwaters of the Tang Chhu appeared; of the mountains forming an amphitheatre, the most prominent were Binamdakha and Chitsukgang, both about 18,000 feet high. They looked impressive and large owing to the new mantle of snow they had acquired after the previous night's storm.

We ascended steadily towards the Pele La, lunching at the last water before the pass. Tiny purple primulae grew abundantly; also a bush with a yellow flower like broom. We had previously been indoctrinated with many woeful accounts of snow, ice and freezing winds making the Pele La impassable before March – April. My diary reads: "So the Steele family sailed over the Pele La without problem and entered Central Bhutan. We were immensely pleased but as we dropped down the other side morale seemed to slide. We feel we have crossed our Rubicon. Judith has diarrhoea."

Snow lay on the banks but we were surprised the road was clear as my altimeter read 11,610 feet. The weather this year was quite unusual; the mild winter was much in our favour during the early months but became a grave disadvantage after the break of an early monsoon when we reached the east. Mounds of stones holding poles with prayer flags attached had been placed on the summit of the pass by travellers in gratitude for a safe passage; the bushes were festooned with coloured prayer flags, giving the appearance of Christmas trees. Mist swirled overhead obscuring the view and low cloud brought a chill in the air, so we wrapped the children up in their anoraks, scarves and gloves. Lakpa took Judith on her pony to give Sarah a rest; after a minute or two at a place of gentle incline, I heard a moan from Lakpa and turned in time to see both her and Judith sliding off the pony's back and landing in a ditch half-filled with snow. Lakpa grazed her arm and Judith was more surprised than alarmed but we did not repeat the experiment. Instead Chhimi sometimes changed to ride Lakpa's pony and hold Judith, as he is an expert horseman.

We had now traversed the Black Mountains, a watershed between Western and Central Bhutan. This ridge, according to White, is the focus of a wet zone extending as far as Tongsa, damp being drawn up from the plains through the narrow gorges of the Mangde Chhu, thus accounting for the prevalence of bad weather in this region. We reached a long, flat valley where large herds of yak and goats were grazing. The shelters of their keepers stood higher than our path, at Longtetang, so we did not meet them. Hail began to fall; the trees on the mountainside above us accumulated a white frosting and the cold became intense, making

Adam's hands icy through firmly gripping his rein harness on the slippery descent; we all tried to sing to keep up our spirits. At Rukubi, the first village, we were hoping for a house to stay in to thaw ourselves but instead were shown to some empty cow sheds in a field beyond. Water dripped off the roof on to a fire that we had started with much difficulty under the projecting eaves of the hut. A crisis had arrived. My diary reads:

"Judith has terrible diarrhoea and we have only two clean nappies left. We worked out the number she needs for a five day journey, as she wears them only at night now, but this has thrown our calculations out. Lakpa will never be able to dry them even if she does get them washed. Sarah is exasperated and wonders why we ever left home."

So did I at that cold and miserable moment but dared not say so as I knew that I alone was to blame for our immediate predicament.

I went off to hunt for some kaolin in the medicine box. We carried one small handy box of drugs beside the large trunk of medicines for use in clinics. Judith was pale and ate no supper, so we wrapped her warmly in Sarah's sleeping bag hoping for an improvement in the morning. We all felt low that evening but such feelings thankfully moderate in intensity with the passage of time. I took Adam into my sleeping bag for warmth and we listened to the hail beating down on the flimsy bamboo roof of the hut, wondering if it would keep us dry until morning.

At daybreak a spectacular whiteness of new snow covered the hillsides, giving the woods a soft and fluffy look and lightly powdering the valley floor where we had camped. The sun warmed us through and we stood dressed in our thickest pullovers drinking hot tea and breathing steam like dragons. Our world had changed overnight; we were all happy again and Judith was a little improved.

The path was exquisitely beautiful following the Longte Chhu, which frothed over falls in spate and then flowed peacefully through deep, still pools. Shortly after passing a small chorten at Saduksum ("the triangular shaped place") which marks the boundary of the Wangdu Phodrang and Tongsa regions, we reached the village of Chendebi.

92

A mile further on at Charungkashor we came upon a large white stupa, a religious shrine with a fifty foot high dome placed on a square-tiered pedestal; it stood in an open meadow, surrounded by tall cedars, at the junction of two rivers where the enclosing hills form a small gorge. The shape of the stupa is similar to Swayambunath in Kathmandu. We were surprised to find such a graceful thing in this sparsely populated valley.

Our path maintained its height, traversing at about 8,000 feet through woods of oak, magnolia, rhododendron and chestnut. As we came round the mountain side the river fell further and further away below us, racing to meet the Mangde Chhu, which flows south from Tongsa and is one of the three largest rivers of Bhutan. We camped at Banglapoktok beside a stream. I wrote in my diary that night:

"It has been a good day. Judith is better and everyone is happy. The children are becoming more adventurous and wander off together while we cook lunch or help the pony-men pitch camp. It is hard to believe that we are in one of the wildest parts of the Himalayas."

Our technique and routine of travel developed as the days passed. We insisted that the kitchen basket should be carried by the man leading Sarah's or Adam's pony, so we could stop and brew tea without being dependent on the baggage ponies, which usually followed some distance behind. I kept fit running between Adam, with whom I held long and earnest discussions on a multitude of topics, and Judith, who occasionally needed to be lifted down to piddle. Despite the string round her neck she frequently dropped her dummy, which I had to retrieve as it was essential for her quiet morning sleep. We soon lost most of our stock, dropped on the path and stamped on by the horses' hooves; eventually we had to manage with only one. After a quick wipe on the seat of my trousers and with faith in the antiseptic properties of human saliva, I pushed it back into Judith's mouth and she appeared quite happy

We lunched at Tsangkha above Tangsebi. Such halts provided a pleasant diversion and we made sure that they lasted at least two hours, so the day was split up into two four-hour periods – quite long enough travelling for young children. The unloaded

93

Tibetan beauty
Goitre patient

ponies were sent off to graze, Sarah and Lakpa cooked a big meal of rice and dal with dried peas and I wrote my diary. The children hurled their metal plates down the steep grass hillside to see how far they would slither and then encouraged the ponymen to chase after them, causing both parties endless mirth.

I had some anxiety for what the afternoon would hold. In 1908 White described the descent to the Mangde Chhu thus: "The gorge being flanked on either side of huge precipices . . . as it descends the road becomes a series of steep zig-zags, mostly made up of stone steps." The name is Thumadak "the place in the rock" – an apt description. The road plunges a thousand feet down a perpendicular cliff to the foot of the gorge. Hundreds of steps carved out of the steep rock wind in a crazy fashion through bushes and trees, that cling to the barren face. These steps had been remade a year previously for the passing of the Paro Penlop on his tour of inspection.

"The ponies must go down first," said Chhimi. "If one of them slips and rolls on us we go quickly into the river. Misses and Lakpa go together and we take the children."

We watched the ponies slowly and carefully descending below us; away in the distance Tongsa Dzong stood like a fairy castle on a spit of land at the junction of two clefts in the valley. I could see Chhimi through the foliage away below me carrying Judith tied on to his back with his dzong scarf; Sarah and Lakpa walked together carrying the ice axes as walking sticks. Adam and I sat watching them and admired the vertiginous panorama before us; then we set off down the rocky ladder holding hands. We could hear the clip-clop of the ponies' hooves on the rocks below and the encouraging shouts of the ponymen helping them negotiate the lower reaches. Such heights, which were our daily experience, had ceased to worry us. Later Sarah remounted and showed her skilled horsemanship on several short flights of steps carved from the river bank; she leaned back and stood in her stirrups clutching Judith to her chest. Adam rocked and rolled in time with the pony's movements; he needed much less help than early on and actively resented the assistance I tried to provide dancing along the rocks on the outside edge of the narrow path to avoid being knocked off by the bedding rolls.

"This must surely be the world's most exciting pony trek," commented Sarah, who is not given to wild exaggeration.

We crossed the torrent by a covered cantilever bridge and climbed nine hundred feet through beechwoods to Tongsa Dzong towering above us. We halted beside a tall prayer flag before the walls of the dzong, where travellers must dismount. The main road from West to East Bhutan enters the massive iron-studded wooden gates of the dzong and passes through its very courtyards, there being no way of skirting the vertical walls of rock on which the dzong is built. This impregnable position accounts for the fact that, during the past century, of all the warring penlops of Bhutan, the Tongsa Penlop who gave origin to the present royal dynasty became the most powerful.

Lamas of Tongsa

## CHAPTER 10

Our caravan passed through the main gate of Tongsa Dzong into a dark gatehouse and then out into a courtyard surrounded by painted balconies. Twilight was gathering and an eerie silence hung over the empty yard. The noise of our ponies' hooves on the paving stones resounded from the enclosing walls attracting a group of young lamas, who peered at us inquisitively from an upper landing. The lofty towers of the dzong loomed above us. Before entering another dark passage we passed the heavily barred dungeon gate being unlocked by a warder for a prisoner wearing leg irons. At the end of the passage we emerged under the fortified walls on the east side of the dzong where the main part of the village was built beside a stream.

Like a fantastic castle out of the Middle Ages, the walls on this side were about three hundred yards long; the whole enormous building sat astride a narrow tongue of land, its roofs at many different levels. Two small stalls and a shop stood beside a mill, from whence water ran on to turn a gigantic creaking prayer-drum, six feet high, set in a small chorten.

Chhimi went ahead to meet Dasho Thrimpon, who emerged from his house to greet us. We were directed to the enclosure of the King's house set a quarter of a mile upstream from the village. Two very tall pine trees dwarfed the house, which stood in its own fenced grounds commanding a superb view over the village houses to the dzong. We decided to occupy a little out-house kitchen; we used one room for cooking and eating, the other for sleeping.

Unpacking our luggage after a week of continuous travelling gave us pleasure. The journey had not been arduous but we were all tired and looked forward to ten days settled in one place. Our little house had shutters on the windows; there was no chimney so the rooms were perpetually full of smoke. We borrowed a large copper vat from Dasho Thrimpon, used for brewing rakshi spirits, and placed it over a log fire to heat enough water for bathing. The luxury of steeping ourselves in soothing hot water was intense, not to mention its cleansing properties, which changed us all to a lighter shade. The children splashed about with glee. Lakpa produced plastic bags full of dirty clothes accumulated on the journey and busily got on with the mountainous task of washing them. A spring from the hillside, passing through a chorten, was excellent for rinsing clothes and provided us with pure drinking water. Chhimi went to the dzong to arrange with Dasho Thrimpon for supplies of firewood, milk and eggs to be delivered to the house.

Our first morning was utterly lazy; having accustomed ourselves to rising at 4.30 – 5.00 a.m. on the road, to lie in bed until eight o'clock was pure delight. I cooked porridge, made a pot of tea and we all went back to sleep again. On sliding back the shutters we saw a beautiful sight: the dzong rose above a ruff of morning mist that hung round its base and drifted up from the valleys; the sun cresting a hill to the east cast a soft light on the massive long white wall of the fortress; behind lay the Black Mountains, Joudung Shing, diaphanous through the haze of the middle distance.

Already a small crowd was gathering, some for medicines, some merely to stare. Chhimi and I dressed to pay our official call on Dasho Thrimpon in the dzong. This time we took a calendar entitled "Castles of Scotland", which provided a topic for conversation as the appearances of our feudal castles bear a close resemblance to the dzongs of Bhutan.

The Tongsa region suited my purpose for carrying out a detailed goitre survey. Endemic goitre has long been recognised as a disease, particularly, but not exclusively, of mountain regions. The name goitre means an enlargement of the thyroid gland which lies straddled across the neck and produces a hormone, or chemical messenger, that controls many activities throughout the body. Iodine is an essential requirement, albeit in very tiny quantities, for the manufacture of thyroid hormone by the gland. When the iodine present in the diet is insufficient the thyroid gland has a natural way of increasing the number of its cells by multiplication in order to present a larger surface area to "trap" any iodine circulating in the blood. The infinitesimal amount of iodine we require comes from the soil, mainly through drinking water. However, the soil of the great mountain ranges and old glaciated regions far from the sea has become gradually leached of its iodine, owing to the latter's ready solubility in water. Goitre is unknown in places where the diet consists mainly of sea food because fish, and seaweeds in particular, have a high content of iodine.

But iodine lack is not the whole story of endemic goitre although it seems to be the most important factor. Anything which interferes with or "blocks" the normal uptake or "trapping" of iodine may cause a goitre to develop in a gland just maintaining its balance. For example, certain foodstuffs block iodine uptake. Second, the element calcium may combine with iodine to form an unabsorbed colloidal substance; goitre was common in limestone districts in England where the disease was known as "Derbyshire neck". Third, pollution of drinking water by human excreta has been proved to cause goitre. Fourth, genetic factors may influence goitre production; one pair of such factors is the ability or inability to taste a chemical compound Phenylthiourea (P.T.C.); statistically it is found that the non-tasters have a slightly increased liability to develop nodular goitres.

In my survey I wanted to estimate the incidence of goitre across Bhutan and to compare this with other Himalayan regions, to classify the goitres according to their shape and size, to investigate drinking water for pollution, to do blood tests to estimate the amount of iodine present and to compare this with the Phenyl-thiourea taster or non-taster status.

Finally, I must discuss the matter of treatment, for to visit some distant part of the world following an academic trail after a common disease with obscure origins is a useless pastime if the sufferers are offered no treatment in return; unsophisticated people are frequently used merely as guinea pigs in the interests of science, from which they personally reap little benefit. Addition of iodine to the diet can prevent goitre and in most countries of the world iodine is added to all the marketed table salt under strict govern-mental control. This explains why endemic goitre is almost non-existent in young people in the Alps where the incidence used to be very high. Taking the chemical potassium iodide by mouth, eating seaweed and even painting the neck with tincture of iodine are successful in preventing goitre.

I was interested in attempting some treatment for already exist-ing goitres. I had read of a team of Australian doctors who had been injecting iodised oil into goitrous natives of New Guinea. They observed a significant regression of all forms of goitre in sixty out of sixty-one patients three months after a single four millilitre injection of iodised oil, and found that this dose pro-vided a sufficient iodine requirement for two to three years. This seemed a worthwhile line of treatment to investigate in Bhutan. Large and longstanding goitres are only amenable to surgical treatment in well equipped hospitals where blood transfusions are readily available, and these will not come the way of the ordinary Bhutanese peasant for some time ahead. I discovered that the New Zealand team in Solo Khumbu were also using iodised oil treatment with success. The oil is injected deep into the muscles where it acts as a depot and the iodine is then slowly released into the blood.

As I explained in an earlier chapter, this goitre survey was only a small part of the medical work. My main commission was to collect blood specimens to be sent back to England for Dr. Mourant and Professor Lehmann of Cambridge to carry out their studies on blood groups and abnormal haemoglobins. The ethical side of this matter also concerned me deeply. I could not go into an area where people rarely, if ever, have an opportunity of seeing a doctor, in order to persuade them to give a blood sample, without offering anything in return. The idea of paying money for blood, as sadly has been extensively practised elsewhere, seemed equally undesirable. When a doctor follows into an area where money has been paid he finds extreme difficulty in dissociating medicine and injections from hard cash, to the disadvantage of both giver and receiver.

I determined to carry out general medical clinics wherever I went and to take blood samples from any of my patients who were willing. I would add that, later on in Bumthang, patients came to my clinic with arms bared, pleading with me to take their blood and examine it; I have no doubt they gained some psychosomatic benefit from this – "the needle is mightier than the pill" is my confirmed premise in practising basic medicine. I had brought one trunk full of medicines, some supplied by a Swiss drug company to Dr. George Eberle and some from Dr. Roy's government store in Phuntsoling.

Chhimi marshalled the waiting patients on the wall by the King's house and we began our clinic. Sarah did the dressings and injections, while I examined patients and prescribed medicines. Adam was thrilled to be doing doctor's work; he became a real help, looking after blood samples and helping me measure the goitrous necks with a tape. During the first morning a patient came to the clinic with the largest goitre I had ever seen; the swelling, the size of a melon on one side and a grapefruit on the other, bulged over her chest. We devoted each morning to clinical work, leaving the afternoons free for specific goitre work.

I carried out a house-to-house survey of the entire village above the dzong; we visited each house, enquired the number of people living there and the number of people with goitre. Then we examined all the people for thyroid enlargement, noted a detailed family and medical history and took blood samples from every goitre patient. Finally each patient was given an injection of iodised oil by Chhimi, who took his work very seriously and roundly rebuked the patient if he jumped when the needle went in; as Bhutanese skin tends to be tough as hide, considerable force was needed to penetrate it.

This work took a long time and required painstaking documentation. If we discovered that a patient with a goitre was not at home, we had to go off in search of him or wait to catch him when he returned from the fields in the evening.

To reach the houses we had to hop from stone to stone to avoid the dung and mire lying in stagnant pools in the courtyards. The ground floor of each dwelling was exclusively used as a cattle shed or a storehouse. A steep narrow staircase, often made of only a single tree trunk with steps cut in it and having a thin hand rail, led in complete darkness to the upper floor. Plank stairs also were so worn and highly polished they were hazardous to climb. Our feet groped in blackness and we were glad to reach the upper room, which was again dark, the walls and ceiling blackened with wood smoke hanging heavily in the air.

The houses had no chimneys because the wooden slatted roofs would be readily set alight by sparks. The window shutters were usually drawn across to keep out the wind, there being no glass. The dominating feature of the room was the fireplace built of baked clay and standing two feet high, on which two or three cooking pots could be placed, fed by a single fire. Cooking utensils hung on the walls and from the ceiling; furniture was scarce, with maybe a rug on the floor to sit on but no tables or chairs. All the bedding was piled in one corner and rolled out on to the floor at night. One room was usually set aside as a family chapel with effigies placed on an altar where butter lamps burned; this also served as a guest room.

On completing the first house-to-house survey we were surprised to find a comparatively low overall incidence of goitre, a result we substantiated more fully in other areas of Bhutan. We returned to our house in the late afternoon and carefully stored the blood; under ideal circumstances for testing it should have been kept at $4°$ C. from the time of collection until reaching London. I investigated all the possible methods of cooling before we left – vacuum flasks, insulated boxes and paraffin refrigerators, but found they were either too complicated or too heavy for the long distances we needed to carry them. I had carefully measured the day-time and night-time temperatures of glacial rivers and mountain streams, finding that the range was 3 – 9° C. for the rivers and a little higher for the streams. Knowing that ideal conditions could never be exactly adhered to, I selected this method and wrote to Dr. Mourant for approval. I numbered all the tubes with a diamond pencil, corresponding with a record I kept, and Adam carefully placed them in a tin over which the stream water flowed. Thus they were left until the first batch was ready for despatch to England, where Dr. Mourant would test them.

The four major blood groups are A, B, AB and O, but hundreds of subgroups and their subdivisions are known, one of which is the Rhesus group. The genes responsible for the various groups are inherited and by studying the gene frequency in a certain population it is possible to reach some conclusions as to the origin of an existing race from their distant ancestors, a fact that is especially true if the gene that is being traced is a rare one and occurs only in a specific geographical distribution. In the particular case of Bhutan, Dr. Mourant was trying to estimate the relative proportion of genetical characters contributed to their ancestry by the Caucasoid peoples of India on the one hand, and by the Mongoloids and other peoples of central, eastern and south-eastern Asia on the other.

Blood serum had to be decanted from the specimens given by goitre patients. After the test tubes had lain still for a while all the red blood cells settled on the bottom and I drew off the supernatant yellowish fluid with a pipette, placing it in small screw-capped bottles for analysis of the iodine content.

Adam proved to be not only a help but a good companion during these lengthy and often tedious procedures. He maintained a flow of endless questions, mainly rhetorical, which I tried to answer until weariness caused me to turn a deaf ear. Then he would become angry.

"Daddy, why won't you answer me? You're not listening."

"I was a bit but I was doing some thinking on my own," I replied.

"Well, stop thinking and answer *me*," he retorted. Already the gulf that separated me from the family during those trying days of the exams was closing. We were now living so close together and living so vitally as a family that I was more confident of my ability to manage the children and aware of the effort and hard work required to forge a close family unity.

After our work one evening Adam and I went for a walk up the hill to explore the small fort, that had two wings radiating from a central tower. We climbed some ladders to the topmost room behind an old monk, who acted as our guide. Hanging on the wall were some very old helmets of metal, ox-hide shields and large broadswords, which had been in active use by Bhutanese soldiers during the last century, and we saw two cannon balls in the dzong captured from the British during a retaliatory foray in the Bhutan-Dooars wars. A story is told of two British soldiers who were captured and kept in the dungeon of Tongsa Dzong for several months. Sadly none of the history of the dzong has been written down; even the thrimpon's knowledge was sketchy and often whimsical. Certainly bow and arrow warfare was used in internecine struggles until the turn of the century. We looked over the roofs of the big dzong on which the sun was falling and making a variegated pattern of light and shade on the many different levels.

Returning through the woods I made up a story around our visit and held Adam enthralled until we reached home where our supper of rice, potatoes and curry powder sauce was waiting for us. Every other supper had been much the same for the past month, but that evening Sarah had experimented with baking in practice for Adam's and Judith's birthday. She had baked a new loaf in a tin supported on three stones inside another larger tin; we opened a tin of strawberry jam to celebrate and felt like gourmands. Fresh meat was almost unobtainable as animals are seldom killed, in accordance with Buddhist belief. Only when a cow falls down a mountainside or dies of old age can one buy meat; then it is usually cut up and sun-dried and is almost inedible being so near to putrefaction. Occasionally we purchased pork, more fat than lean, as the pig is excluded from the slaughter ban. Many of the patients brought eggs or vegetables as thank-offerings, which were hard to refuse without hurting their generous feelings. These supplies supplemented our monotonous diet.

Shortly after our arrival Sarah became sick; the rest of us had shaken off our colds but Sarah's hung on, deepening to a harsh, chesty cough. She felt wretched and I put her to bed on discovering that her temperature had soared. During the next two days she lay in bed feeling miserable, and unhealthy crackling noises filtered through my stethoscope; she started on a course of the antibiotic tetracycline as she is sensitive to penicillin. Lakpa took the children on walks to allow Sarah as much rest and quiet as possible, while Chhimi and I watched over her. I confess that recriminative thoughts passed through my mind as I tried to work out what would happen should she become more seriously ill. I had a fair stock of medicines, but little imagination was needed to appreciate the multitude of illnesses that would have been outside my limited facilities. Our nearest road was four to five days' march away, then it would take a day and a half by jeep to the nearest airfield; no sick patient would be able to tolerate such a journey. I hastily put these thoughts out of my mind but they had a deep and sobering effect on me.

Sarah's fever came to a climax, then eased; she began to improve and take a little food and to drink a lot. She admitted later that she remembered little of the events of those two days, which were passed in mild delirium; weeks later I still shook with fear when I thought about them. When she was on her feet again I left with Chhimi to survey the villages up the Mangde Chhu and to attempt to discover the source of the headwaters of the river.

Ceremonial Horns

# CHAPTER 11

The compounder from Tongsa, Tsering Kunde, accompanied
Chhimi and me on our tour up the Mangde Chhu. A good-
looking, well-built boy of above average intelligence, he had been
sent out to Kalimpong by the government for a form of nurse's
training at the Charteris Hospital. He was in charge of the dispensary, where he gave out his limited supply of medicines and
injections without any medical supervision; his nearest doctor
contact was in the hospital at Thimphu. He arrived at our house
wearing a fur-lined cap and pointed shoes, a transistor radio hung
from a shoulder strap and in his hand he carried an Indian airline
bag. Such, I thought, was the veneer of civilisation that has
managed to brush off on this basically simple and pleasant fellow.
At his insistence we requested a porter from the dzong to carry
our small amount of baggage. After a delay of more than an hour,
when I was becoming increasingly impatient to get away, the
porter arrived, loaded up our luggage and set off into the distance
at a trot while we three men strolled behind. Ashamed though I
am to admit it, our porter was a woman!

We followed a high path above the river, which takes a broad curving sweep westwards from Tongsa bridge; it then bows round on itself before flowing in a straight line from its source somewhere in that nebulous area in the north, designated Kula Kangri. Reaching Singbi for lunch we were entertained by a dirty and intoxicated old lama, who regaled us with stories of his recent annual visit to the King in Thimphu, where I gathered he passed his time as a court story-teller. His nose dribbled and he periodically wiped it with a corner of his sleeve; bouts of diabolical sniffing and snorting quite upset the otherwise pleasant meal of eggs and chilli sauce.

The afternoon was bright and clear so I made some sketches of the valley and took the necessary bearings to correct the only existing map, which is hopelessly inaccurate. Reaching Gagar by evening we slept in the house of the headman. Chang beer flowed freely and conversation became ribald and merry. My host offered me a blanket to warm my feet and I could not refuse; it was the habitat of a legion of fleas, which plagued me throughout that night by marching unconcernedly over my abdomen and biting me at intervals so that I swelled and itched mercilessly.

I wished to proceed as far up the valley as possible next day in order to study its geography more closely. We followed an attractive path through rhododendron woods where many tiny blue gentian lay in damp, shaded places and where birds abounded. Karshong was the last village from where I looked due north into the upper Mangde Chhu. I could find no record of exploration of this deeply cut gorge, whose steep and thickly forested sides plunged sharply into the river, zig-zagging between intervening ridges. The timber line was high to the ridge tops which looked quite impassable; a bar of snow-capped peaks closed the end of the valley. A pass, the Karchi La, led over the mountains east from here to reach the Dhur Chhu in Bumthang.

With my goitre survey of the villages completed, we turned for home climbing steadily through bamboo jungle towards Taphe Gompa where we planned to pass the night. The lama of the small monastery was a delightful man, friendly and welcoming and he invited us to share his meal. His supplies were limited to a monthly ration from the dzong stores, which he had to collect and hump on his back up to his mountain hermitage. He was given a basic quantity of rice and flour and a small supply of brick tea and sugar; supplements of milk and eggs he was obliged to acquire locally. We offered him some of our food and the prospect of a change from his frugal living thrilled him.

The lama busied himself with preparation of the meal, which we ate seated crosslegged round the hearth. A pot of chillis had been quietly boiling for more than an hour; this he strained and mixed with some green vegetable making a thick sauce to season the large bowl of boiled rice he had placed in the middle of the floor between us. The men each produced a wooden eating bowl from their boku pouch close to their skin. These bowls are made from walnut wood turned on a lathe and coated inside with black lacquer; the rim is usually of silver with an engraved silver base but the most elegant bowls are lined with silver throughout; I had bought one such bowl, a beautiful and practical utensil. They helped themselves to rice by the fistful, squeezing it into a compact ball in the palm of their hands, the chilli sauce was poured into the eating bowls and each rice bullet dipped into this and swallowed. Sucking noises, smacking lips and explosive belches punctuated the silence of serious eating. When the pile of rice was finished they swigged the remainder of the chillis and licked their bowls clean with wide circular sweeps of their tongues. I decided to forgo the chilli sauce, knowing the corrosive effect this has on the Western belly, and contented myself with some fried egg.

Conversation broke forth after supper and, helped by the intoxicant effect of rakshi, mounted in pitch and excitement as the evening changed to night. Kunde, the compounder, showed relief that the tour was soon to be over as he had found the utmost difficulty in maintaining the pace at which Chhimi and I liked to walk.

The lama laid a rug on the floor of the temple next door and insisted I should sleep in this place of honour; I was reluctant to accept from the fact that I shared it with a thirty foot high statue, set against the dank living rock, of the Lord Buddha, who peered at me with a searching eye. I moved my bed hoping he would cease gazing at me so intently but to no avail. My haunted feelings were deepened by several demonic figures adopting weird poses whose shadows, cast by the flickering light of the candle, danced on the wet rock behind. I have no experience of ghostly houses but an hour of this treatment was all I could stand; I moved my bed near the kitchen fireplace in company with my fellows, whose vibrant snores gave fellowship after my silent isolation next door. At 10,200 feet the cold was severe.

Swirling mist shrouded us in the morning confounding my hopes of seeing the panorama of northern mountains from the top of Singethang above us. The old lama we had met at Singbi the day before arrived for breakfast in high spirits, less drunken but still drooling. He regaled us with his uncouth humour and was hilariously funny. I examined his giant-sized hernia amid much ribaldry and advised him to keep away from women as a certain cure, whereupon he said he would prefer not to be cured. He took me to his house in a laurel grove above the monastery to show me a collection of old photographs of royalty dating back two generations. He had evidently been a court favourite for many years and must have provided much uninhibited relief from the serious round of royal duties. We climbed down the hill to Tongsa and found Sarah much improved after a good rest, and the children in high spirits.

Next morning Lakpa brought us tea in bed, as had become an established custom appreciated no less by the children than ourselves. Chhimi slept soundly in the kitchen wrapped in his boku; his job was to frighten away the dogs that broke in at any opportunity to steal our food, but he proved a useless watchman as a dog had rifled the kitchen under his sleeping eye and stolen a cheese given to us as a present in Thimphu. Thereafter we barricaded the door and placed Chhimi hard against it.

I pulled aside the shutters and saw a sight I shall never forget. The morning sun lit up the dzong standing on its rocky pedestal against a backcloth of snow-covered mountains still in dark shadow to the south. A single file of purple robed lamas was climbing the path towards us, spread out over several hundred yards like a winding snake. In front marched the band of young gaylongs playing horns and reed instruments, the chants of their fellows filling the stillness of the glen. Life has been lived thus for centuries and we were now part of this historical drama.

The lamas were coming for their weekly wash at the spring in the royal grounds where they passed a day of relaxation, fooling around naked under the spout, chasing each other across the grass and making music. For one day they shed the burden of their discipline to become plain boys again, free, uninhibited and mischievous. The head lama paid a courtesy visit to us and was pleased to be offered tea, which he drank seated on a wooden box in our kitchen. He was fascinated by Adam's clockwork car speeding around the floor; at first it caused him much alarm as he had never seen such a thing. Adam displayed his prowess as a builder with his wooden construction set and soon made the head lama sit on the floor to help him. Intent on not being outdone, Judith paraded her musical box outside and gathered a large circle of admiring gaylongs, but she suddenly became frightened surrounded by so many strange faces and emitted a piercing howl. The children have friendly natures, Adam being especially brazen, and we have never been bothered with shyness; this causes us some embarrassment if they are too extroverted and forward but on our journey when they were continuously meeting new people these qualities proved a blessing.

On our last evening I intended to send off a batch of one hundred and twenty blood specimens to Dr. Mourant, so much work had to be done in preparation. I separated the serum using a hand centrifuge to spin the test tubes at high speed; as much work was involved in this I suggested to the lamas that they should turn the handle in the same way they revolve their prayer wheels. They were quickly attracted by the idea and formed a queue to take their place for five minute spells at the centrifuge. They sat muttering the prayer "Om mani peme hum" at such speed to keep up with the revolutions that it became abbreviated to "O . . . hum . . . O . . . hum . . . O . . . hum. . . " How much spiritual merit was earned by this was hard to say; prayers were flying like sparks off a grinder's wheel and much merriment was enjoyed by the spectators.

Birka Bahadur, the assistant compounder, offered to help in the transport of the blood specimens. Our problem was to get them to Calcutta, cooled throughout the journey if possible, where I had arranged with British Overseas Airways Corporation for their immediate refrigeration and onward flight to London. Birka Bahadur, a Nepali Drukpa, was going on leave to his home in the southern hills so it was little out of his route to escort the specimens to the nearest airfield. I packed the test tubes carefully into their original tins and sealed them with adhesive tape. I had kept the collected blood specimens in the stream and I hoped the snow would still be lying low enough to use for cooling on the three to four day march to the road-head at Shemgang. But the mildness of the winter had put snow far out of reach and I asked Birka Bahadur to travel as much as possible in the night and to leave the specimens in stream water by day. He adhered closely to this plan much to his own inconvenience. I sent him off with enough money to pay all his expenses and only heard of the complications of his journey when he came over to Bumthang a month later to escort the second batch.

Birka Bahadur's march to Shemgang was uneventful; he found a place in a jeep travelling to the border town of Gelephu and managed to collect snow from shaded wayside culverts when crossing the passes. At Gelephu he bought ice from an hotel and took a train to the nearest airfield, at Dobre, where he discovered that all civil flights had been cancelled and the only traffic operating out of the airfield was the military, who were unwilling to co-operate. He boarded a train to Cooch Behar and took two and a half days to travel one hundred and twenty miles. From his financial accounts I knew he had bought ice at every stop, putting it in the large plastic bags which held the blood specimen tins. At Cooch Behar, Birka Bahadur took the tins to the office of the local airline, who, as I had previously arranged, would freight them on their earliest flight to Calcutta and hand them over immediately to the British Overseas Airways Corporation. To the credit of Birka Bahadur, this batch arrived in London eleven days after despatch from Tongsa. Dr. Mourant reported on them later to me by letter.

Our ten day sojourn in Tongsa being over, we felt well rested and were pleased to be on the road again. Our routine of travelling was quickly restored but we soon realised we had acquired a peculiarly useless bunch of ponymen at Tongsa, and some scrawny beasts. Before cresting the ridge we looked back on the wood and metal patchwork of the dzong roofs far below us in the mist-filled valley. Our path was wide and gentle so we ambled along at the leisurely pace dictated by our slothful steeds and their equally idle owners, who made a poor contrast to the excellent men we had hired for the previous stage. Sarah and I appreciated the freedom of the road again, being able to stop or start as we pleased. Adam liked to dismount for a spell of an hour or so when we walked together in earnest discussion; the exercise did him good and made him tired so he was pleased to get back in his harness and have a short doze. Judith slept much of the time firmly anchored to Sarah by her blanket.

Calamity nearly overtook us when she dropped her dummy on the path. Sarah called me back from the front of the caravan, where Adam was riding, to fetch it. I arrived in time to see a large black crow swooping on it, attracted by the brightness of the yellow plastic. The crow pecked and teased the priceless object and was about to fly off with it when I pelted it with stones, so it hopped to a nearby tree and cawed abuse at me. We had no longer any spares so the loss of Judith's dummy would have meant the difference between contented sucking and fractious waking hours.

In our early days of uncompromising principle and rigid theory, Sarah and I vowed we would never allow a child of ours to suck "one of those disgusting things", but nights of wailing mellowed our avowed intentions, since when we have enjoyed contented children. We needed no further evidence; the matter for us was proven. We debated if we should enter this as an essential item of expedition equipment when completing Judith's application for the Ladies Alpine Club.

At lunchtime we were busy preparing food when suddenly we realised that the children were nowhere to be seen. As we had stopped on a precipitous path I hurried off to hunt for them, enlisting the help of the men. After some anxious moments we discovered them playing houses in a thick bamboo grove up the hillside.

Crossing the Yoto La (11,640 feet), we arrived in a broad

alpine valley surrounded by pine forest and an abundance of rhododendron in bud. Snow lay in the gullies so Adam and I tobogganed down on the seats of our pants shouting in jubilation; Judith was more cautious and kept to the path. The ponymen took little trouble to lead the riding ponies over the difficult rocky places so Sarah dismounted and walked until the path levelled off. Chhimi rode ahead on Lakpa's pony to prepare a lodging for us in Gyetsa. He took much pride in being the vanguard of the party and we encouraged this habit as it was pleasant to reach a village and find a house prepared with all arrangements made for us.

Chhimi had obviously laid plans for making a triumphal entry into his native Bumthang on the next stage. He knew that riding up to the dzong on a pony would make him the envy of all his fellows, especially as he would have to pass by the school he had only recently left. I had no wish to deny him this pleasure; he deserved a reward for the invaluable help he had been on the journey so I promised he could take a pony and leave as early as he wished next day. We found a pleasant dwelling in Gyetsa. My letter to Sarah's parents reads:

"We are sitting in a dark smoke-filled room and some women are brewing spirits in the corner; one of them is baking buckwheat bread in flat cakes on a griddle over the fire. We have just feasted on our first potatoes since Thimphu. The children had fried eggs for their supper and are nearly asleep next door with Lakpa still singing quietly to them; they have been wonderful today, on the move for seven hours walking and riding. Although they were very tired I heard no murmur of complaint, even when they became cold during the last stretch this evening before we arrived. I am very proud of them and of Sarah who takes it all so calmly. The time is just after seven o'clock and we will be going to bed soon as we must be away before five in the morning. Some people might think we are mad but we are supremely happy."

Chhimi was astir before sunrise and I heard the clatter of hoofs receding a short while after. The air was crisp and clear as we left Gyetsa; hoar frost clung to the bushes and the sun flooded the valley melting the white crystal carpet. The gentle climb to the

Kyi Kyi La pass lay through pine woods; resin was seeping from the tree trunks, its smell thick in the air. Spring was astir. At the foot of a bar of hills to the south lay Domkar Dzong, large, remote and empty except for a small standing army of retainers keeping it warm for the whim of any passing royalty. Beyond these hills rose some impressive snow peaks of about 16,000 feet which are crossed by two passes, the Nada La and the Tung Le La.

We rested on the Kyi Kyi La (11,560 feet) and looked down a fertile cultivated valley where a large river, the Kagang Chhu, flowed towards its junction with the Chamkhar Chhu, which drains from Bumthang. Some mouse-hares, little hamster-like creatures, scampered from their holes in an overhanging bank and tamely approached us to eat crumbs that the children put out for them. A beautiful bird with a crimson and black striped hood and red wings flew into the woods. Rounding a corner Sarah, who was in the lead, surprised three large pheasants, which ran off into the bushes; their breasts were a brilliant turquoise colour surmounted by a yellow ruff and an exotic scarlet plume. Similar pheasants, named kalij or monal, are the national emblem of Nepal. Tiny blue gentian grew on the banks and a delicately scented white and pink azalea bush bordered our path, which maintained an altitude of 11–12,000 feet for several miles. We were fully acclimatised and found no breathing difficulties at this modest height.

We passed a family travelling on foot in the same direction as ourselves. The slowness of their progress was due to a little pig also walking over the pass, secured by a harness on the end of a long piece of string.

> *"And there in a wood a Piggy-wig stood,*
> *With a ring at the end of his nose . . ."*

Adam was convulsed in laughter at these lines.

Sarah gave me a sweet, part of our meagre daily ration, to pass up the line to Adam; trying to approach close enough to hand it to him I missed my footing on the rough verge of the path and fell headlong into a ditch. I landed on the point of my chin and suffered a temporary blackout. On coming round I discovered I was lying upside down in wet mud with my rucksack round my neck, pinning me to the ground in an undignified position. On seeing my predicament the ponymen rushed up and started collecting the biscuits I had dropped in my fall and promptly scoffed them. I extricated myself feeling somewhat shaken but unhurt apart from a grazed chin, a bruised arm and some loss of face.

Byakar Dzong, Bumthang

## CHAPTER 12

At the top of the pass, marked by a number of tattered prayer
flags, I saw peak on peak of snow-capped mountains ringing the
horizon in an unbroken line and crowning the Bumthang Valley
stretched out below me. The mountains lay on the border of
Tibet, so far distant I could not identify them, but I knew somewhere in that direction the Monlakarchhung pass cut a way north
to Lhasa. I guessed the highest group was Kula Kangri but none
of these mountains has been mapped. I was looking at the least
explored part of the great Himalayan range where not a single
mountain top has fallen under the foot of man. The thrill of that
moment was intense and I remembered Eric Shipton's words in
*Nanda Devi*:

> "I had a mighty longing ... to wander with a small, self-
> contained party through the labyrinth of unexplored valleys,
> forming our plans to suit the circumstances, climbing peaks
> when opportunity occurred, following up our own topo-
> graphical clues and crossing passes into unknown territory."

In a world shrinking so fast with air travel, where man's in-
quisitiveness is pushing him to every distant corner of the globe,

it was a rare privilege to view this tract of virgin land; not just a few mountains but range upon range as far as the eye could see.

Byakar Dzong, engulfed in pine trees, was built high on a bluff at the edge of the broad valley; long in shape with a high central tower, it looked like a battleship at anchor in a rough sea. As Adam was negotiating a steep passage swaying casually with the roll of the pony, he solemnly pronounced, "It hasn't taken us long to get to this castle, Daddy."

"No," I replied, "and we're going to stay here for several weeks so that you and Judith Jo can have your birthday parties."

"Will I have a cake?" he asked, "and presents?"

"I expect so, if Mummy can make one. But I don't think there are many shops to buy presents."

"Never mind," he said, "do you think there will be a princess at my birthday party?"

"We'll have to see," I hopefully told him. Our bedtime reading came from *Danny Fox*, a story full of castles and princesses, whose vivid reality seemed completely natural to Adam. He regarded our whole journey in a matter-of-fact manner and projected events straight into his stories, making them more exciting to judge by his requests for repeated readings. Judith was too young to appreciate the tales of *Danny Fox* although she enjoyed looking through the pictures of *Peter Rabbit* and attempting to recognise the animals.

As we approached the dzong we heard bells across the valley. A mule train of more than fifty beasts, having unloaded their burdens, was descending from the dzong to stables in the village below. The hillside was alive with caparisoned mules; the leading one of each section bore a coloured flag waving and bobbing as it jolted downhill. The sound of this traffic was pleasant music by comparison with the throaty roar of motor engines to which the modern world is daily subjected.

A mile below the dzong, surrounded by fields, lay Wangdu Chholing Palace. Chhimi met us proudly at the dzong to tell us we were expected, Paro Penlop having sent a radio signal ordering everything to be prepared for our arrival. Chhimi wanted me to make a Dasho's entry; he relieved me of my rucksack and, but for my protestations, would have placed me on a horse for the final ride. Approaching the palace we felt as the early travellers must have done on making their entrance to the secret cities of Tibet. We passed a large chorten on our right and entered a walled park through an arched gateway; cherry trees were bursting into flower already, green buds just opening to show their hidden pink petals. An archery ground was laid out to our left beside the path, which led us towards the palace. At the flag pole everyone dismounted and we entered a walled passage leading to the main gateway. The head servant, flanked by his underlings, bowed graciously to Adam and me, who were leading the caravan. Chhimi translated his words:

"My master asked me to make you welcome, Sir. His house is at your disposal and I am at your service."

The change on our ponymen's faces was astonishing when they realised we were guests of royalty and were no longer jesting as they had thought. They busied themselves as never before unpacking our loads and carrying them up to the first floor of the guest house, set in a garden beside the palace walls. The house was quite new, its paintwork still rich and bright. We climbed to the first floor behind Hochen La, the head servant, who showed us in with an obsequious gesture. Large rooms led off either side of the centre dining room each having a small wash-house and privy attached. The ground floor was used for storage, one room being occupied by the palace chowkedar, or gate keeper. Drawing back the shutters we looked up and down the length of this beautiful valley; across a small lawn stood the palace, built like a miniature dzong round a hollow square from the middle of which rose a central tower. Various members of the Paro Penlop's family kept apartments in the palace but it was the principal home of his sister, Ashi Choki. She spends much of her time away in Calcutta or Kalimpong and the palace remains empty for most of the year, maintained in readiness for a royal visit by a full complement of servants.

All our luggage was unloaded and the boxes were carried upstairs. As we intended to spend at least six weeks in Bumthang we decided to unpack everything and see what we had left. We turned a back room into a store and filled the shelves with food, medicine and clothing until it looked as if we were setting up shop. Chhimi was appointed to sleep next door and to be responsible for the safety of the storeroom, which had a large lock and key. He was delighted to have a bedroom to himself. He unpacked and meticulously laid out his possessions: a biro pen and notebook in which he wrote English words, a toothbrush and soap he rarely used and several photos of himself self-conscious and unsmiling standing rigidly to attention.

Everything appeared to be present for our domestic comfort – except a kitchen. With horror we realised that by our sudden ascent in the social scale from itinerants to royal guests we must lose our jealously guarded independence in conformity with the standards expected of us.

"Chhimi, please ask Hochen La if we may see the kitchens," I asked.

"He says they're far away from here. The servants will cook your food and bring it to you," Chhimi replied.

"Please thank him, Chhimi, but tell him Lakpa has to cook the food because English children have delicate stomachs. Flatter him – and please be polite." Chhimi had a manner of bulldozing his way past any obstacle with singular lack of feeling, a technique that proved successful with recalcitrant horsemen but was inappropriate to a man with Hochen La's position. So I reminded Chhimi of his manners.

Hochen La descended the stairs, cleaving a way through the throng of palace servants and villagers who had congregated to inspect the new arrivals. He possessed a handsome dignity that left his authority unchallenged. In appearance like a Mandarin emperor, he was taller than the average Bhutanese and immaculately dressed in a dark blue boku with laundered white cuffs. His face showed the refined lines of a man approaching middle age and on his upper lip grew a small well-groomed moustache. His politeness was so genuine we were loathe to cause any offence after the trouble he had taken with preparations for our well-being. From the house we followed Hochen La down a fenced path to a gatehouse beside the main entrance of the palace, which was kept locked when Ashi was not in residence; crossing a small courtyard we climbed a wall by a rickety ladder and descended some steps on the opposite side into an orchard; turning a corner of the palace we entered another fenced and gated path that led round the edge of the rose garden; we went through another courtyard beside a gompa, crossed some water channels giving power to turn the prayer wheels and entered some low buildings beside the servant's quarters.

"This is the kitchen," said Hochen La. "It is very clean."

Sarah and Lakpa were flabbergasted at the thought of the half mile obstacle course that needed to be negotiated each time they wished to reach the kitchens.

"Do you think there's any chance we could cook nearer the guest house?" I asked Hochen La.

"I'll see," he said, "but we have Bhutanese dinner prepared for you tonight." We returned to the house downhearted that we might have offended him by our outlandish requests but we suddenly saw the funny side of it all – the reluctant royal guests – and burst into laughter.

From our bedroom upstairs we heard sounds of activity rising from the garden area below so we drew back the shutters to observe what was going on. An elderly, bowlegged man with a kind face and soft voice was standing on the perimeter wall directing a large number of workers. We recognised him as the chowkedar, Owya by name, meaning "the fox" in Bumthang dialect. Some men were driving large stakes into the ground, packing their bases with stones and then attaching a framework of thin lengths of split bamboo.

A dozen girls were carrying wooden shingle planks from the opposite side of a kitchen garden where a shack had recently been demolished. Other women appeared from the direction of the village bearing bundles of firewood on their backs and dumped them against the wall. Already a pile of large round stones had been collected from the river a quarter of a mile away and one of the men was carefully positioning them in the centre of the ground-space to form a fireplace. Six strong looking girls were heaving sections of bamboo matting over the garden wall; these they rolled out and secured in place for walls. In less than an hour Owya was putting the finishing touches to a handsome door that swung on bamboo hinges in front of our kitchen.

Adam went down to help supervise the building, fascinated by the speed and skill of its construction. We thanked Owya for his trouble and went in to look round; the hut measured twelve feet by eight and was ideal for our needs. Lakpa lit a fire while we arranged our tin trunks and some wooden boxes round the walls for seats; Sarah hung all our kitchen utensils from nails driven into the supporting stakes and I pinned last year's Christmas cards to the walls for a final touch of decoration. Soon the empty hut was transformed into our home; Chhimi named it "Drungso Chholing" meaning "The doctor's palace", and wrote a sign, which he fixed to the outside of the door.

Hochen La and Owya came to approve the work and we invited them in for tea. The head servant was evidently dismayed at our behaviour and sat on the edge of a box, his attitude formal and composed. Owya refused to be seated in our presence and stood by the door, his cap in hand; each time we addressed him he bowed from the waist; when we passed round the cigarettes he held both hands together and nearly touched the ground in obeisance. This servility worried us at first but we decided to say nothing, hoping it would pass when they came to recognise that we were ordinary mortals.

While we were drinking tea some servants carrying four gallon drums of water on their backs climbed the stairs of the house a few yards away from our kitchen. Twenty loads of hot water had to be carried over the "obstacle course" ending with a steep climb up difficult narrow steps to the little room projecting on piles where an enormous tin bath, four feet long, three feet deep and two feet wide was housed. The whole family clambered in and soaked in blissful, relaxing warmth; never do I remember a more enjoyable bath. Judith was frightened of the water at first, being unused to bathing, but soon she plucked up courage and she and Adam fooled about happily.

We managed to persuade Lakpa to follow us but only after firmly barricading herself inside; she never quite got accustomed to our family's lack of modesty, especially when Adam volunteered to share the bath with her. Despite much exhortation we could not persuade Chhimi of either the pleasures or the necessity of such ablutions.

Next door to the bath was a small room for the thunderbox of unique Bhutanese design; raised one foot off the ground it measured two feet long by six inches wide, and was carved out of solid wood. One sat astride the narrow box, from the bottom of which a square boarded channel led through the floor of the room into the ground below where a large hole had been dug. Considering the lack of running water this pattern of privy was fairly hygienic provided the direction of the wind was favourable.

Clean clothes made us feel fresh after days and nights without changing. We put the children to bed early as they were weary and after sunset the temperature at 9,000 feet fell abruptly. We sat in the centre room awaiting the promised feast, which was announced by the arrival of Hochen La and his clerk, Rinzin, carrying a tray with tea. Rinzin was about twenty years old and had been to school in Bumthang where he had learned to speak and write English; he was a cheerful and openly friendly lad, and carried a notebook wherever he went in the wake of his senior, writing little notes and jotting down figures.

Sarah and I sat in style at the table covered with a laundered white cloth while Chhimi and Lakpa squatted in the shadows after the fashion expected of them. The Bhutanese tea was strong and salty and bore a thick layer of butter droplets on the surface; Sarah had to force herself to drink it but I encouraged her by pointing out that it would taste far worse when cold. We heard noises from outside and looking through the door we saw a procession of lanterns approaching us in the darkness from the direction of the kitchens, accompanied by the rise and fall of voices. Eight servants appeared and were directed to place the trays and pots they carried in appropriate places by Hochen La, who hovered like the head waiter at a state banquet. A large platter of boiled rice was served and we were directed to help ourselves to various bowls placed before us. One contained a kind of broccoli, one potatoes and another a meat stew; our excitement at the prospect of eating meat was dampened as soon as our teeth bit into parts of the various mountain beasts present in the pot. Long strips of dried yak meat had been boiled in an unsuccessful attempt to soften their consistence; the rugose lining of a goat's stomach, though making an attractive honeycomb pattern, proved quite unpalatable. We tried our best to show appreciation to the servants for their trouble but under their watchful eyes in the penumbra it must have seemed a paltry charade. Lakpa and Chhimi, noticing our dilemma, giggled and we had difficulty not to laugh. As soon as we had played out our expected part we thanked Hochen La and the servants, who retired; we ran down to our kitchen, built a huge fire and brewed cocoa. From then on we determined to carry on living together as a family in the way that had so far proved successful.

The following day we settled into our new house. Hochen La visited us at breakfast and accepted a cup of tea but was still bemused by our behaviour, displaying a mixture of curiosity and disdain. However, he quickly warmed to us and remained a good friend for the duration of our stay. He wanted to know our needs regarding milk, eggs and potatoes, which we could buy from the palace storehouse; Rinzin, in attendance, carefully wrote down each item in his notebook. A short while later a lean, athletic looking boy arrived, sent by Hochen La to help in our kitchen. His name was Dolay and he was a good-natured, kind, hard-working boy in whose care I felt confident of leaving the family when I went off on tour. Dolay was recently married to a pretty girl, Nalemo, and they had a three-week-old baby, Daba. He took over the kitchen and ran it on his own lines, leaving Lakpa free to do the washing and look after Judith.

Sarah, Adam and I made our formal call on the thrimpon in the dzong about a mile away. We first walked across fields and then climbed steeply through the village of Byakar. A zig-zag path rose to the dzong at whose massive gates Chhimi's uncle, Dasho Thrimpon, was waiting to receive us. With this meeting began a close friendship and liaison that enhanced every aspect of our life and work during our sojourn in Bumthang. Dasho Thrimpon was turning forty years of age, quiet and courteous in manner. He had entered the King's service at the age of ten and remained as a servant of the royal palace until he was appointed nyerchen at Byakar Dzong; seven years later he was promoted to thrimpon, one of the most senior posts in Bhutan. In his office on the first floor we drank many cups of tea, three being the minimum in token of politeness and etiquette, and ate sweetened buttered rice brightly tinted with saffron. Dasho Thrimpon showed a detailed interest in our work, promised us any assistance we might need and asked us to call whenever we were passing the dzong.

We returned through the bazaar, which had two shops and half a dozen small stalls run by Tibetans. In most places across Bhutan the traders were Tibetans, the Bhutanese appearing not to have much aptitude for finance. The shops had little to sell; sugar, tea, needles and cotton, packets of gaudy coloured sweet-balls and cheap Indian cigarettes. We were fortunate to have brought with us a few luxuries as none would have been available in Bumthang. The radio station and post office completed the village essentials. We sent a signal to the Paro Penlop reporting our safe arrival and thanking him for his house; then we collected mail from the postmaster, a boy straight out of school who appeared completely bewildered by the responsibilities of his job. His qualification was that he could read but he lacked any sort of experience to give him confidence in handling a post office.

I took Adam and Judith over the field to the bridge across the Chamkhar Chhu. We gathered many stray pieces of wood on our way to provide ammunition for our games. A hundred yards upstream the river was turbulent, then it entered a deep whirlpool below the bridge whence it emptied over a rocky bed. By hurling our sticks high into the white water we could make them gyrate in elegant patterns on reaching the whirlpool. Then they shot under the bridge and we raced to the other side to see whose stick arrived first. I heaved large rocks into the pool, which exploded in white foam, and the children screamed for more. Time flew past unnoticed in this naïve entertainment and we only reached home as darkness was falling and Sarah was becoming anxious.

Roadside House

## CHAPTER 13

Our days formed a pattern into which everyone easily settled so we could hardly believe that Drungso Chholing had not always been our home. Sarah and I have moved so often following from one job to another in medical training that any form of permanence has become unnatural to us. We are convinced that, for the children, home is not built of bricks – nor even bamboo – but is the place where their parents are and where they have security in the family: with these provisos a nomad child can have as fine a home as any suburbanite.

Each morning Lakpa and Chhimi took turns to bring tea to us in bed at about 6 a.m. – a great luxury; Dolay arrived early to tidy the kitchen and boil my shaving water. Porridge or semolina was the mainstay of breakfast. Lakpa cooked roti, flat bread made by heating dough in a frying pan over the fire, which we ate with butter bought from the dzong and our precious jam. Adam and Judith each had a fried egg, as did the adults when they were plentiful.

By 7.30 a.m. I left for the dispensary which was a further half mile up the hill behind the dzong, half to three quarters of an hour away. Whenever possible I took Adam as my companion and helper; he had his own stethoscope and proudly wore it round his neck while assisting me. His pleasure reminded me of my own when as a child of his age I used to help my father in his work as a surgeon. The dispensary was sited in a disadvantageous position far from the hub of life. However, I felt that I should try to centre some of my clinical work on the existing government medical service rather than appear to run a rival concern. The compounders Ugyen and Penjo were manifestly grateful for any teaching I gave them; they led a lonely life hidden away above the town in a place far from their home. Medical supplies were scarce because their annual replacements had been lying at the border town for several months owing to some bureaucratic lack of communication, in spite of repeated requests for forwarding.

Patients waited on the balcony of the dispensary while we worked in comparative comfort within. I treated them, took blood samples where appropriate, and made a record of their diseases.

By midday the work was finished and we came back down the hill to Wangdu Chholing for lunch. This meal rarely varied: a pile of rice, some potatoes fried in butter, occasionally with spring onions, and a little precious mango chutney brought from Calcutta which the children did not like, so we did not try to persuade them to eat it. A little powdered red pepper added flavouring to the otherwise plain meal.

In the afternoon Sarah and I held a clinic upstairs in Chhimi's bedroom where all the medicines were laid out. The patients presented us with all the usual problems of a general practice at home but with certain notable exceptions. Heart disease was surprisingly common in people of younger age groups, due to an untreated attack of rheumatic fever in childhood scarring the valves of the heart, thus rendering them liable to failure in later life. Such patients were usually far gone and my drugs could but temporarily halt a relentless downhill progress.

Leprosy is most common in East Bhutan; to make a diagnosis of leprosy in a patient living in a healthy community is a heart-rending experience as one knows that the victim is condemned to become an outcast and to enter a leprosarium. The tell-tale patches on the skin like ringworm, the loss of sensation in fingers and toes, small unhealing ulcers, bosses on the face giving the characteristic leonine appearance, these are early signs well known to the indigenous people.

I saw several cases of advanced tuberculosis mainly in the elderly but I suspect the disease is more widespread than was diagnostically apparent using my stethoscope alone without X-rays. Unfavourable social conditions of overcrowding, dirt and undernourishment favour the spread of the tubercle bacillus, and these circumstances undoubtedly prevailed in the majority of Bhutanese houses I visited.

Eye disease was common. Cataracts caused blindness in many elderly people who, with facilities for surgery, could be restored from a life of unnecessary darkness to useful vision by removal of their opaque lenses. Among women chronic infection of the lids with soreness of the white of the eyes was common because they spend a large part of their day crowded over wood fires in smoky, airless kitchens; at night they use slivers of pine chippings for illumination and the burning sap gives off an acrid and irritating smoke. They responded well to ointments and bathing with lotion but the precipitating situation was so unavoidable that a long term cure seemed unlikely.

Traumatic injuries also occurred; mauling by bears encountered in the forests, faces torn by backfiring of antiquated muskets and tendons of the foot severed by the ricochet of an axe.

The commonest complaint, which I soon discovered embraced any malaise between the umbilicus and the knee, was gonor-rhoea. Patients complaining of the disease ranged from senior lamas to respectable married women, and although most classes might have had cause to suffer, the genuine occurrence was rarer than claimed and the condition was often no more than a stomach-ache, a hernia or painful micturition. I was unable to discover the origin of this erroneous and unfortunate label. The gonococcus undoubtedly throve among both young and old lamas owing to activities inherent in a monastic life. Promiscuity accounted for the higher incidence among ordinary folk but I doubt if it was any greater than in the Western world. A florid form of syphilis occurred in several patients but the late results of the disease were rare, suggesting that infection has never been prolific.

Gynaecological problems were usually the late results of difficult deliveries carried through without medical assistance. We learnt from an elderly lady who attended the clinic with a monstrous prolapse of her womb, that an Indian doctor had visited Bumthang some years previously. During his brief stay he had seen this lady and by some stroke of genius or magic had produced a ring pessary and had showed her how to use it to maintain her womb in place. Faithful to the instructions the doctor had given her, she was one day washing her ring in the stream beside her house and performing her ablutions when an important male visitor arrived. Covered in confusion she dropped her device and rushed indoors to prepare tea after the expected custom. Suddenly she remembered with horror her priceless possession and ran out of the house in time to see a mangey dog disappearing over the wall with it between his teeth. Since that day no doctor had been in Bumthang and no pessaries had come her way either. The tragi-comical irony of the story caused us to burst out laughing.

Children suffered mainly from diseases due to poor hygiene; impetigo, worms, discharging ears and bronchitic snuffles. While we were in Bumthang a measles outbreak occurred in the region and more than thirty children died; this reminded me of the serious implications of such an epidemic in a people with little or no previous immunity. On the whole Bhutanese people were healthy and possessed an extra-ordinary stoicism in the face of pain.

Sarah did all the injections and dressings, allowing me to see a large number of patients. She also took over the small gatehouse near the archery ground at the entry to the palace grounds and ran it as a small hospital where four patients could be housed. The relatives came too and camped alongside, providing food and welfare. Among her hospital patients were a woman with pneumonia on both sides of her chest, the pregnant wife of a policeman with an ovarian abscess and a threatened abortion, and a desperately ill child with measles.

Sarah held a dressings clinic in the morning; her two most successful patients were a lama, who came with a foul discharging carbuncle on his back, and a young boy whose toe, severed by a knife, we sewed back in place. During the clinics we were assisted by a little Tibetan lama, who was a refugee living in a house in Wangdu Chholing village. He had fallen down the steps of the Potala in Lhasa when he was a boy of twelve and had broken his spine, causing him thereafter to be hunchbacked. His centre teeth were missing and two side ones projected over his lower lip, which always beamed in a smile. On his head he wore a red hat, the earpieces of which were turned upwards like a mediaeval court jester's. He visited us on any excuse and having discovered that I had a Tibetan medical dictionary, would hurry up and down the line of waiting patients taking histories and presenting us with many a bizarre picture of the complaints they claimed to be suffering from. We could not resist his charm and boyish humour even if his translations were misleading.

I frequently stood back and thought, "What are we really achieving by all this?" I have always regarded peripatetic medicine with a sneaking suspicion; drifting into a community with the air of a guardian angel, handing out pills and potions on the strength of snap diagnoses and passing on, leaving many forlorn hopes shattered and faith destroyed. In a transient encounter little can be done in the way of curative medicine except perhaps pulling rotten teeth or incising ripe abscesses. Cynicism is easy; much less easy is to see what form of doctoring can begin to meet the needs of a people who have never had contact with modern medicine. Of the latter the Bhutanese are highly mistrustful; when ill they prefer to call in lamas or magicians, who for a fee will recite prayers or perform witchcraft with the aim of dispossessing the patient of the evil spirits that afflict them. I do not mean to pour scorn on such practices; in a country where the nearest doctor is a good ten days' march away, what other recourse have people in the anxiety and distress of sickness? On occasions I was called to see patients who had been ill for several days attended by the unceasing incantations of the lamas, but only in the last resort had they called me although they knew perfectly well that a doctor was in the vicinity.

Sarah and I both felt that although our efforts could be nothing more than a temporary stop-gap, perhaps this was a small step forward on the road of educating the people towards accepting modern medical facilities that one hopes will reach them in the not too distant future. We trusted that some impression would be made on them by a doctor examining them carefully, by a nurse kneeling down and cleaning their filthy sores, by our visiting old people in their houses and attending patiently to the children. Such menial labour is not thought worthy of the Dasho class of society in this feudally impregnated system and it was undoubtedly a revelation to patients that Sarah was happy to perform the dirty jobs required of her in the course of her nursing.

By the end of our time at Bumthang the lama's back had healed completely, the woman with pneumonia walked a day's march home on her own and the boy with the severed toe was running around playing at archery. Their gratitude was obvious and we knew that some good had come out of our labour, albeit a drop in an ocean. I remembered the words of a missionary doctor I had met in India, who was coping with a population approaching a million in the neighbourhood of his hospital.

"You cannot hope to solve the problem, but at least you can show how the problem may be solved."

Clinics were fun but tiring; by late afternoon we were glad to retire to the peace of our kitchen and sit round the fire. Part of our problem was language; I was getting on tolerably well with Dzonkar, the national tongue spoken especially in the west, and was compiling a vocabulary and phrase book as no written Bhutanese language book is available. However, as soon as we entered Bumthang a completely different dialect was spoken, bearing no resemblance to Dzonkar. I carried on compiling my vocabulary using both languages side by side but my progress was slow and I never felt I had got to grips with it. I was disappointed with my efforts as I have a reasonably good ear for languages inherited from my grandfather, who was a scholar in Chinese, Hebrew and Gaelic. Perhaps my greatest problem was living in such close proximity with Chhimi, whose English was improving rapidly and who could not understand my desire to speak Bhutanese. Seclusion from one's native tongue helps in learning a new language, as there is no escape from speaking and thinking in the foreign way. A basic comprehension of grammar is essential as a structure on which to build and this I found difficult to acquire.

In the evenings we had a stream of visitors, who called in to sit and watch, to drink tea or to talk. We kept open house and throughout the day a kettle was on the boil brewing tea, with dire depletion of our stocks of tea and sugar. Evening was the time for discussion; we would ask questions about every aspect of Bhutanese people's lives in order to build up as comprehensive a picture as possible. Hochen La came, always perfect in manners, never sitting until invited, observing every courtesy; never did he drop his austere and formal air which gave him the quality of a model butler and valet. Rinzin was more exuberant, more boyish; he enjoyed company and for hours on end would gamble with Dolay, Chhimi and Leppo using dice and beans as counters laid out in a complicated geometrical pattern on a board. Oaths and ecstatic shrieks would punctuate moments of silent concentration. Leppo, also one of the palace servants, was the bow and arrow maker in his spare time when not attending to his job of supervising the stonemasons; short and muscular, his bullet-shaped head resting heavily on a thick neck and broad shoulders, he had the rudest sense of humour of all our visitors. Obscene giggles so convulsed him that he rolled off his box on to the floor which caused the others to howl with laughter regardless of Leppo's joke, and hysterical guffaws resounded from our small kitchen. Presiding in a seat of honour beside the fire, for he was our most regular visitor and also most senior in age, sat Owya the Fox. Adam called him Danny Fox and the name stuck, causing much amusement to the assembled men when they saw the illustrations of the exploits of Danny Fox and the Princess in Adam's book. Owya's boku was becoming threadbare and his knee-length Bhutanese boots had holes through which protruded the moss he used as an insole padding. He was a palace servant through and through, loyal to his absentee landlord, and a very genial man.

The establishment was run on feudal lines; Ashi Choki comes

to Wangdu Chholing for a month or two each year and in her absence the palace is maintained by a band of servants under the direction of Hochen La. They receive no wages but may, from time to time, be given pocket money by their mistress; each are provided with essential foodstuffs and two new boku a year; their wives also weave for Ashi, who sells the cloth in Calcutta. Besides the permanent palace staff, everyone in Wangdu Chhoing village is obliged to do a certain amount of work for the palace – cutting wood, hauling water or gardening.

During the latter part of our time a message arrived telling Hochen La that Ashi's return was imminent; activity in the palace rose to fever pitch. Owya escorted groups of women round the grounds brushing up dead leaves and raking gravel paths. Thirty men were employed in putting up a new prayer flag at the entrance gate, the old one having faded in the weather and the wind. The pole was lowered by means of ropes and a new hole dug for the base; the forty-foot-long flag, freshly stamped from woodcut blocks with black ink, was tacked into position. When the pole was ready to be hauled up a lama blessed it with prayers and built a little fire of pine needles whose smoke gave off incense and the men heaved on the ropes while Hochen La and Leppo directed the base into its hole. A group of stonemasons were busy erecting a water chorten beside the two already standing near the back gate of the palace. A high plinth was first built in stone brought from the river on the backs of women; on this stood a small temple, six feet square, with one entrance door. The stream flowing through the kitchen yard was diverted to run down a channel into the back of the chorten where the water ran over angled paddles fixed to the base of the six foot high drum that was turned on a central pivot. Thus, night and day, the drum revolved emitting prayers unceasingly. Sacred texts were painted in high letters all the way round the mighty wheel, which in turn was packed with thousands of pieces of paper on which prayers were written. At each cycle of the wheel a bell clanged announcing the sending out of another burst of devotion into the ether. The water ran out through phallic spouts on the front of the plinth, where the villagers filled their buckets. The masons' skill in dry stone walling was of high quality; one old man, evidently the master-mason, was directing operations.

Standing beside a group of workers resting for a break on a pile of stone, was a little boy of Adam's age; his head was thrown backwards, his eyes closed, and he swayed as if in a trance. I thought for a moment the child was having an attack of epilepsy as he did not respond when his father called him; we watched him with fascination for several minutes then he stirred, awoke and began to cry as does any child on waking from a sound sleep. We questioned the father, who said that the boy was so used to accompanying him into the fields and woods that he had developed the habit of sleeping on his feet which he found more convenient and comfortable than lying down on rough ground. Certainly the child appeared quite normal when he had shaken off his sleepiness.

Weavers

## CHAPTER 14

Living in Wangdu Chholing gave us a chance to observe the work of the villagers in their daily round and to form a picture of their economy. The season of the year was beautiful; the fruit trees were in blossom, deep pink and cerise contrasting with the delicate yellow-green of the willows just bursting into leaf; spring was approaching and men were hard at work preparing the fields for sowing.

At the altitude of Bumthang rice is not grown, its upper limit being around 7,000 feet. The staple diet is buckwheat which is ground into coarse flour, made into round cakes and baked in the fire embers. The consistence is doughy and I found the taste repulsive, being accustomed to eating rice, which is a luxury for Bumthang people as it has to be imported from Tongsa or the south and the cost is prohibitive for the ordinary peasant.

The Bumthang Valley is broad and fertile but the methods of cultivation are so primitive that barely enough food is grown to feed the local population. Fields are tilled either by hand, using a mattock followed by raking, or ploughed. Two oxen are harnessed by a broad yoke from the centre of which a beam leads to the wooden share controlled with a curved handle by the farmer. The implement is heavy and cumbersome and ploughs to only a shallow depth. The fields are small and cut up by irrigation channels fed by streams flowing off the hillsides. As water is plentiful, irrigation is easy and all the available valley floor is under cultivation.

Ash made by burning wood chippings and dead foliage provides the main source of fertiliser as no chemicals are available; cow dung is dried into cakes and used for fuel and manure is scarce as the herds are small. A few small tractors could transform this valley and hopefully the day will soon come when the road reaches Bumthang and mechanised farming follows in its wake. Many ills of civilisation will doubtless follow after the road but that is no reason to keep these people in picturesque isolation when their standard of living could be so improved by contact with the modern world.

Wheat grain is sown but the quality of seed is poor. In the palace gardens a good crop of potatoes was being grown; vegetables were scarce solely owing to lack of suitable seed. The government is spending a lot of money developing fruit farming in the valley and many hundreds of trees have been planted under the supervision of the department of agriculture. The altitude and climate are well suited to fruit of all kinds, apple, pear, cherry and plum, as was evident from the prolific blossom in every part of the valley. If the trees are in good production when the road reaches Bumthang in four to five years' time, fruit could be easily exported south to India, giving a boost to the local economy.

Milk is scarce and of poor quality owing to the difficulty of grazing the cows that have to feed off the higher alps among grassless forests, as the valley is fully used for cultivation of wheat. No grass is grown for fodder, hay is scarce and there are no artificial foodstuffs; consequently the cows are lean, mountaineering creatures with small udders that produce limited quantities of milk. Most of this is churned into butter and is not drunk straight even by the children, much to their disadvantage in early post-weaning years. Sarah tried hard to educate the mothers on this aspect of child care and to encourage them to use mixed feeding of cow's milk and solids when the children were taken off the breast.

As the Bhutanese are Buddhists animals are not allowed to be slaughtered either for food or because of old age or disease, therefore the problem of building up a well-bred herd will always be difficult to overcome. Only when cattle die or are killed by falling down a mountainside is the carcass used for meat; the flesh is cut in long strips and laid out to dry in the sun; when hard as leather thongs it is stored away and will keep indefinitely.

Yaks live only in the high mountain pastures along the northern borders at an altitude over 10,000 feet. They are hardy creatures, very agile and strong for transport over mountain passes but of no use in the lower climes. The female cross-bred dzo produces milk and its meat is much favoured.

Pigs are found in the yards of all houses, a black long-bristled species whose flesh escapes religious sanctions and may be eaten. Goats feed on the mountain sides and produce some milk but flocks are small; this is fortunate as timber is quickly ruined by goats chewing the bark off trees. Chickens run loose, living off scraps and producing small eggs; no attempt is made to farm them owing to lack of feeding stuffs.

Our impression of the agriculture of the valley was that enormous potential existed but it was limited by lack of mechanical equipment and the poor quality of seed and fertiliser.

At the far end of the village two carpenters were working on a house using timber from a derelict building. They each used an axe, kept razor sharp, a hand adze and a simple cross-saw. The wooden beam framework of the house was cut and all the joints carefully measured on the ground; when every piece was prepared and marked a gang of men appeared and, under the directing eye of the old carpenter, proceeded to assemble the beams like a child's building kit so that in the space of a few hours the bones of the house were in place without a nail having been hammered. All Bhutanese buildings depend solely on close-fitting joints and occasional wooden pegs for security. The craftsmanship was of a similar standard to that seen at Thimphu Dzong but the construction details were easier to follow on the smaller scale.

Bhutanese men are farmers, builders, carpenters and masons, but time is never so precious that they cannot shoot in an archery match or stop for a drink of chang or a game of dice. By comparison women are the beasts of burden and heavy labour accounts for their haggard features, from which feminine beauty is so commonly absent. On one occasion when we were sharing out the baggage two women porters appeared to have far the heaviest loads; I pointed this out to two of the largest men in the group, who replied, "Yes, they have to work by day while we need to keep our strength for the night." Their womanly occupation is weaving on looms erected in the porches of their homes. The handwoven cloth of eastern Bhutan is famous; as well as providing material for many boku and kira throughout the country, it is taken to Calcutta and sold. The women work all day squatting in front of their looms, which are fixed upright to the wall, with a belt support around their back keeping the weave taut.

Bhutanese women are subordinates in a man's world accepting their lot without complaint, for they can do little to improve their position. Men visiting our house evidently considered my demonstrations of respect and affection for Sarah to be quite strange. One day Dolay's wife, Nalemo, brought their baby, Daba, for a family photo; with much persuasion Dolay sat beside Nalemo, placing his arm round her shoulder, and was greeted by hoots of coarse mirth from the onlooking men. When it was suggested Dolay should kiss his wife he was overcome with a mixture of horror and confusion but eventually agreed amid raucous applause. Dolay and Nalemo appeared more devoted to each other than any other married couple we met but the suggestion that they should show their affection in public was quite unacceptable. However, it appears that no lack of physical contact exists between the sexes, as women have a succession of pregnancies with little interval for recuperation.

Marriage is an informal contract. Girls are eligible from about the age of sixteen onwards; the match is made commonly by choice or by mutual arrangement between the parents. The couple live together and have children, which is the visible seal of a marriage; they may then go to the dzong to be formally registered, but this is not essential though useful should there be a divorce later. No lamas or religious ritual are necessary and the whole matter seems to fall into place with little fuss or ceremony. Polyandry was frequently reported by the earlier travellers in Bhutan but we saw no evidence of it. We found polygamy practised mainly among the wealthier classes as a matter of economy rather than expediency. The commonest form of polygamy is for a man to marry two sisters, as did the present King's father and also the thrimpon of Byakar. Dasho's senior wife, the elder sister, stayed in Chhume to look after the large family estate and her five children; the younger sister lived with him in the dzong and looked after her sister's children who were old enough to be sent to Bumthang school; she was then expecting her own first child. This arrangement seemed to work admirably. A similar situation was present in Nepal where Gurkha soldiers away from their farms on mercenary service needed one wife to keep the farm in order at home and another to travel with them to supply home comforts. We found a block in the minds of some missionary brethren in comprehending this fundamental social and economic fact of life. As in other parts of the world, wives are expensive things and so the privileged classes are the rich. One dasho in the east of Bhutan had seventeen children, ten of whom were in Tashigang school at one time.

Divorce is a simple though costly matter, consequently only the wealthy can afford it. Either party can decide on a separation but the party that so chooses must pay compensation ranging from one hundred rupees to seven hundred rupees to the opposite party, and the divorce must be registered.

Although the Bhutanese attitude towards women and marriage is outwardly casual their interest in sex amounts to an obsession. Phallic symbols adorn the balustrades of bridges, they are carved in the form of water spouts and painted in vivid colours, they appear suspended by string from under the eaves at the four corners of houses pierced – I never could discover why – by a dagger. Chhimi exemplified this preoccupation by always talking about sex. He beat up his fried eggs assuring us that if he ate them with the yolks unbroken he would have terrible trouble with his "important thing". So each time we cooked eggs, as happened nearly every day, Chhimi would wait till last and fry his own, beating them vigorously and making rude suggestions the while. Sarah and I became quite accustomed to the interest that was shown in the intimacies of our own life, but we liked the Bhutanese lack of inhibition and found the rudeness of their humour much akin to our own.

The women are seldom free from the burden of pregnancy; childbirth is a gamble that sometimes produces a live infant but frequently fails to do so, or the child dies soon afterwards. To say that life is cheap in such countries is naïve and unfeeling. I believe the sadness that is felt at the loss of children is equally deeply shared by women all over the world however developed their society may be; it happens that some, by repeated tragedy, become inured to the sorrow of it as a natural defence.

While I was away on a tour of the villages Sarah was called to Hochen La's wife, who had gone into labour; progress was slow with distress developing in mother and baby. Sarah went with much trepidation, her knowledge of midwifery being a little rusty, and was told the ghastly tale of the woman's two previous labours that had lasted five and three days respectively, and was assured that this one was showing signs of taking a similar course. The baby felt high in the abdomen and seemed to be lying transversely. Sarah went back to our kitchen to collect some sleeping pills to give the poor woman a temporary rest and for a cigarette to calm her own nerves. On her return a few minutes later she found the lady delivering, kneeling on the bed and resting on her elbows, a logical and practical position for delivery we had not come across before. Sarah heaved a sigh of relief and helped the young midwife, a competent girl from the new mother's own village, bath the baby who was by now crying vigorously. Sarah gained enormous prestige from her laying-on of hands, presumed by all to have been the factor producing this speedy and successful outcome, and every time she called to admire the new baby she was plied with cups of tea in gratitude.

After delivery the placenta was buried or put into the river and the mother was cleaned and dressed in new clothes. In the subsequent days she had three baths a day prepared by Hochen

La in a deep carved-out log with heated river stones placed in it to maintain the temperature of the water, to which herbs and spices were added. The bathing took place behind a bamboo screen in the yard where snow lay on the ground beside. A queen continues bathing for twenty-five days and other women according to their social status; Hochen La's wife bathed for fifteen days.

Babies go straight on to the breast provided the mother has enough milk. We met a girl whose first three children died because she had too little milk and only when the fourth was born did she find a friend, whose child had died and who therefore had plenty of milk, who was able to feed the new baby instead. The women have no knowledge of the use of dried milk and fresh milk is scarcely available. After a week they feed a mixture of butter and sugar to the baby as well as breast milk, and continue so long as the mother is lactating or until the next baby comes along. Weaning is haphazard; often the grandfather helps by chewing bread or wheat porridge into a soft consistency then taking it from his own mouth on the end of a grimy finger and placing the food gob on the baby's tongue. Provided a child can overcome the vicissitudes of the first year or two he has a good chance of reaching adult life. Under the squalid conditions they are reared in – picking their food off the floor shared with mangey dogs, rarely free of running noses and discharging ears, and lacking immunity to the common exanthemata of childhood – it is surprising that they survive at all.

In old age the Bhutanese have the support of their families among whom, contrary to current Western custom, they are permitted to die in peace. Death is merely an incident in the wheel of life turning towards a new reincarnation, the form of which will be governed by the merits or demerits of the person's life. For the mourners, Chhimi assured me, it is a costly business and more expensive than a wedding.

I watched a funeral on the banks of a river with Chhimi explaining what was happening. The corpse was laid on a large pile of firewood shrouded in a white cloth. In many places firewood itself was scarce, requiring to be brought from considerable distances down the mountainsides as the law forbade the cutting of timber within sight of the dzong, a ruling aimed at preserving the forests in the neighbourhood of habitation. Beside the pyre a large tent was erected for the feast and to shelter the lamas, who are hired to pray for the soul of the deceased. The social status of the family dictates the number of lamas hired and the duration of their prayers. A poor family will only have one lama praying for ten days; a wealthy family hires as many as one hundred for a maximum of forty-nine days – but I never fathomed the significance of this number. A senior lama commands three rupees a day, a middle-class lama two rupees and an ordinary monk one rupee. They must be supplied with food twice a day, porridge once a day and tea five times; for this they pray from sunrise to sunset with the other members of the family. For three years the family meet on the anniversary of the death to pray for three days. The enormous expense involved may easily be reckoned. The pyre is finally lit, the body burned and the ashes cast into the river, so bringing to a close a cycle in the wheel of life.

Our sojourn among the Bhutanese people was so brief that the observations I have made on their social customs could scarcely be anything but superficial; nor do I claim that they are authoritative, they are either my impressions of scenes we witnessed or records of what we were told by Bhutanese themselves.

On the first day of spring, March 21st, we awoke to find six inches of snow had fallen during the night. A brilliant white carpet lay over the valley, the branches of the willow trees were weighed down and bent over and snow lay heavily on the cherry blossom. The dzong looked like a fairy princess's castle standing high above us; the snowdusted forest behind and cloud swirling round its base made it appear to hang in air. It was also Adam's birthday but we decided to keep quiet and have a combined party for him and Judith before we left Bumthang. The snow put aside for a few days any thoughts of going north to Monlakarchhung, so I decided to go off on tour with Chhimi in an attempt to complete the goitre survey and blood collection.

The snow disappeared from the valley almost as quickly as it came, allowing us just enough time to build an enormous snowman outside our kitchen, which was dressed up in old clothes by Dolay. I knew the snow would persist for longer in the high mountains where I wanted to go; even during this brief storm all the passes leading out of Bumthang were closed. I met two men suffering from snowblindness having struggled over the Kyi Kyi La through soft snow that reached to their armpits. All the mail routes were temporarily closed and the postmaster reckoned it would take several days before the mail runners would get through unless we had long periods of sunshine.

With one porter, Kunzong from Naspe, we walked for half a day up the Chamkhar Chhu and then forked east towards the Phe Phe La, which crosses into the valley of the Tang Chhu. We bivouaced under a tree in thick mist at 10,800 feet having built a bonfire to keep ourselves warm. I had a sleeping bag but the boys were only wrapped in their boku.

"I sleep anywhere. I'm a Bhutanese man," said Chhimi when I enquired if he was comfortable, "when I was a boy looking after horses on the mountain I always slept out. Never fear."

Despite the rain dripping through the foliage I felt happy to be in the open beside a stream and the flickering flame of the log fire. I thought of Whymper's poetic descriptions of his bivouacs in the Alps:

". . . and shortly afterwards, as it was getting dark, I encamped in a lovely hole – a cavity or kind of basin in the earth with a stream on one side, a rock to windward, and some broken branches close to hand. Nothing could be more perfect: rock, hole, wood, and water. After making a roaring fire, I nestled in my blanket bag . . . a brilliant meteor sailed across full sixty degrees of the cloudless sky, leaving a trail of light behind which lasted for several seconds. It was the herald of a splendid spectacle. Stars fell by hundreds; and not dimmed by intervening vapours, they sparkled with greater brightness than Sirius in our damp climate."

A light dusting of snow lay on the Phe Phe La (11,880 feet) when we crossed next morning. On the further side the path dropped steeply through bamboo scrub opening out on to yak pastures where we met an old man walking to Byakar Dzong with his four year old son. Further on we encountered a pretty girl carrying a huge load.

"Where are you going?" she asked.

"We're off to the high mountains," Kunzong replied.

"Don't go up there," she said, "or your testicles will swell up so you can't climb." This was greeted with raucous laughter by the boys.

"I've been up in the high mountains and I'm all right," said Chhimi. "I'll show you." He was convulsed with his own ribaldry and the boys continued to shout at the maiden, vulgar exchanges echoing across the mountainside as she climbed the hill.

We breakfasted at Takhung on potatoes and butter tea and pushed on walking at speed past Chutte towards Thodak, at the head of the valley where the Doyong Chhu meets the Tang Chhu. We climbed hundreds of steps cut out of the cliff to the monastery of Thodak set on the face of a rock precipice a thousand feet above the valley. In the gompa, where a large cave was carved from the rock, some monks were wrapping silk covers round old books, numbering several hundred priceless volumes. I particularly wished to discover if a way led out of the Tang Chhu to the north; over supper I found my answer by plying the youngest of the monks with questions as he had walked all over the region. A small path apparently leads to a yak pasture at Soka and then follows several passes to Nashamlung ending, after a journey of five days, at the border by Darmalung, which lies at the head of the Kur Chhu north of Lhuntsi. Kunzong had also passed this route earlier and confirmed what the young monk said. All this geographical information I carefully recorded in a notebook and on my return I asked a clerk in the dzong to write all the place names in Tibetan script so that the correct spelling could be later worked out by scholars in London.

We followed down the Tang Chhu past Urchen Chholing and spent the night at Bebzur; we crossed the Bata La (10,360 feet) next morning arriving back in the Byakar Valley after an absence of four days. The boys had walked hard and we had covered a remarkable amount of ground in the short time carrying out clinics at all our halting places.

I had received the King's permission for Eric Shipton's entry to Bhutan and had cabled to his postal address at the Royal Geographical Society two weeks before. I had heard no word from him but decided to stand by our arrangement of April 1st as the deadline for his arrival in Bumthang, because I was much looking forward to his companionship on the trip to Monlakarchhung.

Having a few days of March still in hand, I went on another brief tour with Dasho Thrimpon to his home village of Chhume in a neighbouring valley one day to the south. He proved an excellent host and was manifestly grateful to me for doing clinics among his people, towards whom he showed a sincere concern and affection. Although our communication had to be mainly through Chhimi's interpretation apart from my faltering phrases of Bhutanese, I felt I had established a close friendship with Dasho and I found him a deeply sympathetic character.

On my return to Drungso Chholing there was still no news of Eric Shipton so Chhimi and I set about our preparations to go north to Monlakarchhung. We chose enough food for ten days and packed our warmest clothing; we were poorly equipped for a high altitude expedition but considered it merely as a reconnaissance.

On the day before we left a train of seventy mules arrived from the south; we could hear their bells and see the following cloud of dust from several miles away. A Tibetan princess, also having the title Ashi, had been away shopping in Calcutta and was returning a few days later; these animals bore her purchases. At the rear of the caravan rode her two children escorted by a bodyguard of strong men, bandoleered and armed with shotguns and pistols. The children were approximately the same age as Adam and Judith and we were pleased that they would have some playmates at last.

Kuje Monastery

## CHAPTER 15

On the orders of Dasho Thrimpon two porters arrived early on
April 1st, the day of our departure for Monlakarchhung. I
requested that Kunzong should accompany us again as he
had proved a success on the Tang Chhu tour; he brought along
Wangdu, a friend from his village of Naspe. Although the snow
had gone from the valley floor we had received gloomy reports
the previous day from a group of yak drivers who had driven
their caravan down from Tshampa; they said snow still blocked
all the passes north and they had only just managed to drive their
yaks through the gorge. There seemed no point in delaying
further as the weather had been changeable since the big snowfall
of March, and was now deteriorating. The pattern was unusual
for the two months before the monsoon, which are generally
fine and settled. We seemed to be paying for the mild weather
of February, so much in our favour during the early days of our
journey. I suspected the storm of March 21st heralded the
monsoon almost two months early, and subsequent days proved
that I was right.

Chhimi had been looking forward to this day for weeks and by now considered himself a mountaineer; wearing a woollen balaclava bearing a badge of the Dalai Lama and armed with an ice axe always in his hand, he looked the part. For a week prior to our departure he suffered a bout of acute lethargy and laziness but the threat of being left behind goaded him into activity. I was warned by Dr. Tobgyel about "certain irregularities" when he occasionally lapsed into such moods; I thought these were probably the result of spending long days alone looking after horses on the hills during his boyhood, with no one to talk to and nothing to do but lapse into a mental vacuum. When he had plenty to keep him busy Chhimi was a tower of strength and activity, but when life was slack he slid into a semi-comatose state from which he could be shaken only by severe reprimand. Never did he resent this nor hold any grudge; Sarah and I loved him and appreciated all he did to ensure the smooth passage of our life.

We said goodbye to Sarah, who was intending to spend a few quiet days of domesticity with Lakpa and the children in preparation for the next stage of the journey east. We followed the left bank of the Chamkhar Chhu through wide fields until we reached the monastery of Kuje, the summer residence of the Tongsa lamas, who migrate there annually. The large three-storeyed building stands on an escarpment above a bend in the river, backing against a small rocky outcrop. The windows in the upper storey were larger and projected in bigger bays than those below, the general appearance being more developed than any other domestic building I had seen. At the confluence of the Kur Chhu and the Chamkhar Chhu we crossed the river by a log bridge and then walked on to Thangbi, where we lunched at the shack of a Tibetan silversmith. He had recently finished making a beautiful short Bhutanese knife with the traditional finely worked silver handle and a razor-sharp blade; after long discussion I persuaded him to sell the knife to me at a reasonable price. His reputation as a maker of arrow-heads stood high so we bought several as presents and also some attractive small ladles made from a metal alloy.

We were about to leave the Tibetan's shack when Dolay

arrived out of breath, bearing a note from Sarah that read, "Adam has a needle in his foot, please can you come." The porters were walking ahead of us so I told Chhimi to catch them up and take them on to Naspe, where they should wait for me. Dolay was very tired having run all the way, so I thanked him for the wonderful effort he had made in catching me and asked him to rest and return at his leisure bringing my rucksack.

Then I ran and ran, reaching Wangdu Chholing nearly two hours later, during which time fearsome thoughts went through my mind. To remove a broken fragment of needle from soft tissue is a notoriously difficult task even under X-ray control with full surgical facilities. The prospect of having to anaesthetise my own son and operate on him appalled me.

I arrived to find that Sarah had extracted the complete needle and Adam was curled up in her arms looking pale and whimpering but in no pain. Sarah told me what had happened: Adam was running about the garden by our kitchen in a brand new pair of Bhutanese boots, of which he was inordinately proud. One of the disposable needles I had used for collecting blood must have been carelessly dropped from the rubbish box when it was being emptied and was lying in the grass. The inch and a half long needle pierced the sole of Adam's boot when he trod on it, passing right through from one side of his foot to the other. Luckily, a small plastic guard attached to one end of the needle halted it and Sarah was able to pull it out unbroken, relieving the poor boy's agony. During the rest of the day he lay quietly in a bed we made on the wooden boxes beside the fire and never complained. We were anxious about tetanus but as there had apparently never been a case in the valley, and as no antitoxin was available anyway, we put the thought out of our minds. We started to treat Adam prophylactically with the one bottle of penicillin syrup we possessed, carefully preserved for such an occasion, and Sarah and I took turns to read to him. By evening he had perked up and was feeling himself again. I was very glad Sarah had recalled me as we were able to discuss the matter together thereby relieving her worry.

The following morning Adam's foot was already healing. In case of emergency I arranged with Sarah to send a radio signal to the Bhutanese army post at Khakthang, from where a runner could be sent to reach me. I then left at speed to catch up with Chhimi and the porters at Naspe, a day's journey away. At Nganghlakhang I halted to see the woman whom Sarah had nursed through pneumonia; her chest emitted not a crackle and the patient felt completely cured.

I reached Naspe in the late afternoon and met Chhimi.

"Where are the porters?" I asked him.

"They thought you wouldn't be back for several days. Kunzong has gone to his cattle pasture and Wangdu is visiting a relative in Kharsa," he replied. "I told them not to go."

We managed to force the lock of the house where our gear was stored and I pressed two passing soldiers into helping us carry the loads on to the army camp at Khakthang. Meanwhile I sent Chhimi off to search for the boys with orders to bring them to Khakthang by nightfall.

Arriving at the camp an hour later I was given a friendly welcome by the lieutenant in charge, who invited me into his house for tea. While we were exchanging courtesies I noticed a bow in the corner.

"I see you've a fine bow there. Do you get much chance for shooting?" I asked.

"Yes, it's the only pastime we have," he said. "Have you ever shot a Bhutanese bow?"

"I've done a little at Wangdu Chholing," I replied, "but I've never hit the target. It's a great sport."

"Then you'd like a game," he suggested, getting up and walking to the door. He roared "Dachaba", the sound echoing across the parade ground to the barrack rooms. Men poured out of their quarters at this summons to arms as if preparing to meet a foreign intruder; within a few minutes I was in the thick of an archery match being treated as the honoured guest. At first I was overawed to be shooting with such experts but the politeness of the soldiers allayed my qualms and I threw myself into the contest with vigour. The ground was shorter than Wangdu Chholing so I tended to overshoot but I began to find a length as darkness drew in, bringing our impromptu match to a close. At the same time Chhimi, Kunzong and Wangdu appeared; we cooked a hearty supper and settled in early. In the middle of the night I went outside to pass water and was surprised when the huge Tibetan mastiff guard-dog, now unchained, bounded over towards me. I just gained the hut in time and slammed the door in its face.

Soon after leaving the camp at Khakthang in the darkness of the following morning, we entered a deep ravine. High crags on both sides plunged to the river and in many places the narrow path abutted on vertical rock. I could imagine a platoon of marksmen positioned here holding up an army attempting to invade from the north. Our road climbed and fell, hugging the contours of bluffs and hanging over culverts by the width of two logs a hundred feet above the swirling torrent, which dashed its tempestuous way south towards the lazy valleys. In this sombre and claustrophobic place rhododendrons were in bloom giving a dash of vivid scarlet and soft pink, carpets of purple primulae lay beside the path and the heavy scent of a small white azalea bush filled the air.

We stopped for lunch at Gongzam and crossed the river by several small bridges connecting rocky islands; here the gorge relented for a space. We basked in the sun on a pleasant meadow and cooked some strips of dried meat. We had brought large supplies of chura, tsampa and churpi. Chura is prepared by heating fried rice slowly in a large copper bowl; the rice swells and when dry is put into cups of tea by the handful. In Bumthang we became so partial to chura that the children always demanded it with their tea, which made a nutritious drink. Tsampa is a finely ground barley eaten especially by Tibetans; some of the flour is poured on to the top of a bowl of butter tea and mixed slowly with the finger, which is licked at intervals until a soft porridge is formed. I found tsampa much less to my liking than chura. Churpi is an excellent hard ration; cheese is beaten and dried to rock-like consistence and then strung in small squares on a piece of string like a necklace. Churpi cannot be bitten into but must be kept in a corner of the mouth and slowly gnawed away until the outer rind softens enough to scale off a little cheese; one piece may last an hour or more and I found it refreshing and a pleasant taste.

148

Adam making friends
Carefree days

The path continued to switchback during the afternoon and the dark walled ravine became more oppressive as heavy clouds obscured the sun, casting a dismal dullness on the atmosphere. A narrow valley opened to the west revealing a massive amphitheatre of snow-covered spires towering thousands of feet above us like alpine pinnacles and many isolated sentinels standing free from the main rock formation. The break in the monotony of the enclosing walls was only momentary and we were plunged again into the narrows of the gorge. Four hours after leaving Gongzam we burst out on to a green sward of yak pasture where two rivers, the Monlungphu Chhu and the Chhuthang Chhu, met. The place was called Pangyetanka and just beyond it stands the isolated military post at Tshampa. We made a fire in the gatehouse, beside which I erected my tent. The evening was dark, snow fell gently and at 12,450 feet the cold was intense.

A Tibetan yak herdsman called in to talk, inviting us to visit his hut after we had eaten. We later followed his directions, crossing a small bridge and stumbling in pitch darkness along a path beside the river, which we could hear thundering below us. Approaching the lights of the yakherd's shelter we were greeted by the fierce barking of dogs; the boys were terrified and climbed a nearby rock, entreating me to follow.

"They will eat us," Chhimi assured me, "I have seen a man eaten by these Tibetan dogs, sir, I'm afraid to be eaten." We stood on a rocky island in the dark brandishing sticks against our unseen enemy. The yakherd called to us that we were safe to approach; as we passed him holding the chained dogs on a short lead, I appreciated the boys' fear. These large black Tibetan mastiffs looked somewhat like bears with their long sharp teeth and vicious growls. We sat beside the fire in his low roofed house and heard his story.

He had been a farmer in Tibet until seven years before when the Chinese policies became unbearable. He had crossed the border with his brother, who had decided to leave Tibet after all his teeth had been knocked out with a rifle butt by the Chinese soldiers he was feeding in his house. They fled south with his brother's family and two of the children had died from exposure sleeping in the snow on the top of a high pass.

149

A carpenter

His job was to tend the large herd of yak belonging to the Tibetan princess in Bumthang and to move them between grazing pastures according to the season of the year. He was given his clothes and rations but no pay; until a few months before, when he was joined by a young nephew, he had lived alone in this desolate place. He told us tales of life in Tibet and seemed pleased with our company. Chhimi bought a three weeks old mastiff puppy for fifteen rupees from the old man who promised to guard the dog for us until we returned from the mountains.

Sunrise next morning was spectacular. A lofty snow-capped peak loomed over Tshampa making us realise we had arrived in the heart of the great mountains. We followed the Chhuthang Chhu for three hours, more and more peaks appearing in the morning sunshine. By the time we reached Waithang the clouds were closing in and snow was falling. The tree line ceased at this point where my altimeter read 14,000 feet, only a few scrubby bushes breaking up the barren, rocky valley. The wind rose up and blew snow harshly in our faces finding its way through to our shirts. I sent Wangdu back to Tshampa in case a message should come from Sarah, as I was still anxious about Adam's foot. After a good meal that put new resolve into us, Chhimi, Kunzong and I pressed on up the valley reaching Chhuthang (15,100 feet) two hours later. The afternoon storm set in and we were unable to see any mountains, the cloud base being down at valley level. We found a small hut measuring twelve feet by six feet, with a roof but no door or windows; snow lay deep on the floor drifting into the corners. Outside we found some buried planks which we laid to make a floor, then we barricaded the wall openings as best we could. We were joined by two Bhutanese soldiers on border patrol and the five of us worked together to make the small hut windproof.

The blizzard was gathering force and snow was blowing horizontally at speed like spin-drift. We climbed onto the roof in order to rearrange the timber slats, then we filled cracks in the walls with stones from a nearby stream. Our labour warmed us and soon our shelter became comparatively weather-proof; the whole scene reminded me of sitting out storms while dog-teaming in the wastes of Labrador four years before. The temperature fell with the approach of night and registered twenty-five degrees below zero centigrade. Snow swirled outside and the wind howled like a pack of wolves, a lonely, empty wail. We huddled round the fire built in a corner of the hut, ate a good meal and settled down to try to sleep.

I have never spent a more miserable night. At first I lay listening to the vehement turmoil around us. Here was I, surrounded by many unexplored, unclimbed mountains; would the storm abate enough to afford me a glimpse of them? After such effort to reach this goal, it was tantalising to be in the midst of such plenty yet unable to see beyond an arm's length. Our food was limited and I knew we could not sit out the storm indefinitely; the rate at which snow was piling up outside revealed the possibility that we could be cut off in this very remote and inhospitable place. Meagre consolation came from the knowledge that I had reached nearer to Lhasa than any other foreigner since the Chinese invasion of Tibet. The Holy City lay little more than a hundred miles due north of me; there stood the Potala, the Norbulingka, the great monasteries of Drepung, Sera and Ganden – thoughts too tantalising to dwell on.

I drifted into a fitful doze and awoke two hours later. My watch showed 9 p.m.; still another eight hours till dawn. As the wind had changed direction I was covered with a powdering of snow, and fine particles were gusting through chinks in the window boarding. I shook out my sleeping bag and moved towards the fire, which had died to embers; I split some wood and stoked up a blaze to cheer and warm myself. Shoving Chhimi over I wedged myself between him and Kunzong for warmth, disturbing the profound sleep of neither. Around Kunzong floated a harsh, unsavoury odour that I deemed worth suffering for the heat I gained from the proximity of his unwashed body. Again I dozed off but this time I was plagued by dreams and awoke in a cold sweat feeling violently sick. Sleeplessness and dreaming are induced by altitude but I did not think I was sufficiently high to be worried by them.

My first dream was that I had perforated my appendix – long since removed – and required an urgent operation. As we were stuck in this hut, Sarah was summoned and I awoke on seeing her standing over me sharpening her scalpel. This was followed by dreaming that Adam had developed tetanus from his wounded foot and I was running madly towards Wangdu Chholing, tripping over every few yards. Finally, I had an audience with the King, in the person of Hochen La, who threw all my blood specimens out of the window saying that I had stolen them.

I woke again at 3 a.m.; the snow had stopped. The howling of the wind had died, leaving an eerie stillness after the tempest. I emerged from a hideous nightmare into a miraculous dawn. Outside the sky was full of stars and beautiful ghostly shapes of the distant mountains of Monlakarchhung stood before us. A foot of new snow lay on the ground covering every mountain, hill and valley in a magnificent white mantle.

We built an enormous blaze to thaw out our frozen limbs and to warm our blood; I cooked a bowl of porridge for Chhimi and me, which we washed down with a steaming mug of sweet coffee and chura to give us energy for the day's work. I sent Kunzong down to Waithang to prepare food for our return later in the day. As we left the hut at Chhuthang, now almost submerged in drift, the sun was rising and touching the summits of all the surrounding peaks as if gently waking them to life; moments later as it crested a hill to the east the valley was flooded with light and the mountains at the head stood out in royal magnificence that only winter can give.

Chhimi and I walked for an hour northwards along the valley looking for a place to cross the fast flowing river; all the boulders we might have used for hopping across were covered with ice and I was loath to get our feet wet so early as the cold was still biting. Eventually we found a division of the streams and managed with some difficulty to leap across using boulders as stepping stones and to clamber up the further bank overhung with icicles, treacherous but beautiful. From our position I decided to climb the mountain due east of Chhuthang that offered a gradual slope on our side and promised to be a focal point for viewing the peaks in the region. The sun had not yet reached the foot of the mountain and the gullies were filled with crisp snow allowing me to kick steps up the first one thousand feet. This was hard work but gave a pleasurable feeling as my heavy boots bit into firm snow which held so I could step up and kick again without sliding back. Chhimi followed easily in my steps, emitting grunts of pleasure at his first real encounter with a big mountain. From the gulley we emerged into a flat shoulder of ground and looked across a small frozen lake to the apex cone of the mountain, rising another thousand feet above us. Now there was warmth in the air and the sun was beginning to melt the firm snow crust so our steps broke through into soft snow. The crust would appear to hold, but on transferring our body weight to the forward foot, there would be a crunch and the boot would sink up to the knee into soft snow lying beneath. Even though it was before 7 a.m., the sun's rays were strong enough to weaken the surface. We quickly put on our snow goggles to avoid the intense glare from the myriad frozen ice crystals. We halted a while to eat some sweets and take a brief glimpse of the view but hurriedly decided to push on before the sun should further damage our climbing surface.

Three hundred feet below the top more troubles began. Massive boulders over which our route lay were covered with new snow, obscuring the crevices with pockets full of soft drift. Stepping from snow-covered rock to rock was firm underfoot, but sometimes I misjudged the texture of the surface and fell headlong into snow up to my neck, requiring much effort to extricate myself. The altitude was beginning to make its effects felt and my energy and determination flagged. Sitting at the bottom of a hole with snow down my neck and in my boots, dishonourable thoughts permeated my addled and anoxic brain that throbbed like a drum keeping time with my pulse, and my breathing became laboured so that I panted.

"Why the hell bother with all this sweat just for a few hundred extra feet? Who is going to know if I don't get to the top? Chhimi would be thankful to go down right now and photos will look just as good from here. I wish the storm had continued and I had never left that fire at Chhuthang. Why come climbing anyway? I suppose I have to justify myself to the Mount Everest Foundation. What a labour just to see a few old snow-covered mountains!" Such are the vagaries of the mind that threatened my moments of high climax and made me ashamed to call myself a mountaineer. I remembered an identical occasion six years before, a few hundred feet below the crater's edge of Popocatepetl when I was dragging a tired old Mexican guide called Sancho up the mountain on the end of my rope, he being even more exhausted than I was. I felt like death but kept going because I wanted to send a postcard to Sarah, then my girl friend, to say that I had climbed the mountain with the most beautiful name in the world. But now some weary, dreary minutes later the dazzling wonder of the summit views broke on me, putting all unworthy thoughts to flight.

Chhimi and I sat on the knife edge crest at 17,080 feet, looking at a panorama of the biggest mountain peaks of Bhutan: one of the great moments of my life. Our climb was a very modest feat by Himalayan mountaineering standards but the truth dawned on us that we were probably the first people ever to see the hundreds of mountain tops laid out before us.

Several spectacular peaks of 20–23,000 feet lay along the Tibetan border; to the west was one markedly higher than its neighbours, named Kula Kangri on all available maps; but this is the name of a mountain on the Tibetan side and is not known as such in Bhutan. A spire-shaped peak seemed to correspond with Rinchita, seen by Ward from the Lunana side. To the north I could see the glacier leading from the Monlakarch-hung La and the lake Pamoi Tsho, the last camping ground before crossing the pass. This used to be the old trade route between Central Bhutan and Lhasa; rice, flour and betel nut passing north, while wool and salt came south.

I gave names descriptive of their shape to the most prominent mountains and drew a sketch map of the region. From The Pyramid (Chisangri) and The Mitre in the centre of my picture, a hanging glacier broke on to a long sharp-spined moraine that curved sinuously towards Chhuthang between us and the Black Peak. With my Abne level I estimated the height of the Mon-lakarchhung La to be about 17,500 feet. In every quadrant of the compass I saw unclimbed mountains, a scene of snowy vastness that offered unlimited possibilities for exploration.

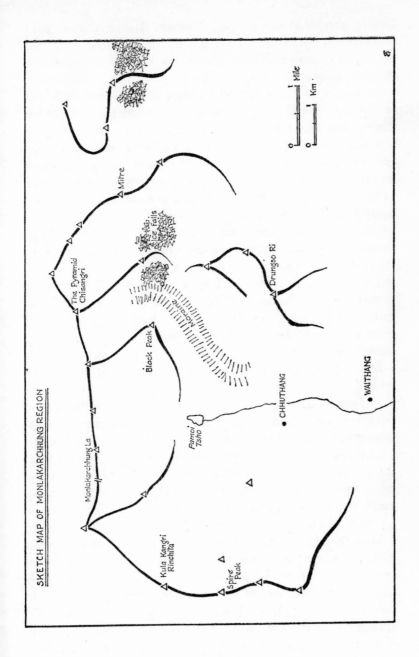

SKETCH MAP OF MONLAKARCHHUNG REGION

Chhimi decided to call our peak Drungso Ri, meaning doctor's mountain in Bhutanese. I suspect, under less snow, it would have been a simple climb but it had proved a hard struggle for us in the existing conditions.

By 9.30 a.m. the snow had softened to a horrible slush and clouds were building up in the south, announcing the midday storm. On the descent Chhimi became very frightened; in our hurry to get off the mountain I made him glissade, or toboggan, on the seat of his pants down the smooth snow slopes, using his ice axe as a brake. At one place where we were forced to take to the rocks I tripped in a hidden hole and crashed down about thirty feet. The soles of my boots must have collected a cake of packed snow causing me to slip off the rock; I tumbled headlong, slewed round, crashed my leg against a rock and shot over a small ledge. I managed to ram my ice axe in before I gathered uncontrollable momentum but the force of my fall and the twisting motion snapped the shaft. When I came to rest I lay still and gathered my thoughts. For one very frightening moment I thought I had broken my leg as the pain was exquisite; having recently exhorted Chhimi to avoid such a catastrophe I felt a fool sitting immobile in the snow, but I was only badly bruised.

We glissaded most of the last thousand feet down the gullies; this spared me walking on my leg, which was becoming increasingly painful as the numbness wore off. By midday we reached Chhuthang and drank some hot coffee from the Thermos flask, ate a packet of biscuits and set off back to Waithang as the morning snowstorm was starting. I found great relief by changing out of my heavy climbing boots into my soft and light Labrador sealskins. Kunzong had prepared lunch and we wolfed it down.

Menacing clouds hung about us as we left Waithang in swirling snow and bitter cold. I was tolerably comfortable so long as we kept moving but my leg stiffened up at each rest halt. I missed my sealskin gloves, one of which had been stolen by a foul dog that had broken into our house at Wangdu Chholing and disappeared over the wall with it in his mouth. Sealskin has many advantages in high altitude clothing; with a lining of duffle it is impermeable to cold, wind and water, becoming softer and more

Owya
Rinzin

pliable when wet; the boots are comfortable for padding around camp and with several pairs of socks, and duffle or deerskin slippers, would carry a pair of crampons with ease; the gloves with duffle mitten inners allow good manipulation of an ice axe and rope. I also wore my dark blue Eskimo sillapak, or anorak, made of windproof Grenfell cloth over my down duvet jacket; the silver fox lining of the hood kept out most of the weather.

We took three hours to reach Tshampa, having to cross three unpleasant landslides on the way down; they seemed much more frightening now that I was tired than on the outward journey. We found Wangdu sitting beside a fire in our little gatehouse, a welcome haven in the miserable dark evening. We had rested for only a few minutes during the previous sixteen hours and were fatigued to the point of exhaustion. But what a day it had been! In Chhimi's and my memory it will shine as one of the outstanding days of our lifetime.

I slept soundly in my tent while much new snow fell during the night. We only just finished our climb in time as the weather seemed to be deteriorating fast. My leg was stiff but much less painful than I had expected. After a quick breakfast Chhimi and I called on the Tibetan yakherd to collect the puppy, which had been branded on his forehead with a piece of red sealing wax indicating his purebred ancestry. He was an endearing, furry black creature, and Chhimi called him Drungso. We made a bed of lichen and moss for him in the top of my rucksack and set off at a fast pace, leaving the porters to follow with the loads in their own time.

We met a fairyland beauty in the gorge. Trees were laden with snow; the sun breaking through the foliage cast shafts of light that reflected brightly off the white carpet; a light steam rose from sun-touched patches of snow forming a gentle haze; large flakes fell melting from the trees and flower blooms were bent over by the weight of snow. The river tumbled wildly, resounding booms echoed from the cliff walls in the ravine and the hills above pointed high into heaven. We maintained our pace and I soon forgot the discomfort of my bruised leg; three hours later we reached Gongzam where we cooked rice and dal and drank several mugs of sweet coffee. Drungso had a run about, relieved

Above Tshampa
Chhimi near Monlakarchhung

himself and ate some rice. We raced on down the gorge and the hours sped past.

"If we reach Wangdu Chholing tonight you can have two days' holiday to visit home," I told Chhimi.

"I have been thinking so," he said with a cheerful grin. I remembered the marathon walk I had done in less than forty-eight hours from Jomosom on the Nepal-Tibet border down the Kali Gandaki to Pokhara, where Sarah was waiting, while I was coming round the north of Dhaulagiri. Then and now I had that triumphant feeling of knowing the work was accomplished and with nothing to linger for but to speed homewards. To feel fit and strong gives a sense of wellbeing quite unparalleled in my experience.

By the time we reached Naspe we were tiring but we kept on going to Thangbi where we made some coffee on the hearth of the Tibetan blacksmith, who was away from his home. With handfuls of chura the hot drink put new life into us and we set off on the last leg home. Chhimi and I reached Wangdu Chholing just eleven and a half hours after leaving Tshampa – normally a two day mail runner's journey. On top of the past few days of strenuous work this achievement set the seal on our comradeship. Sarah was surprised but pleased to see us and Adam was running around without bother from his foot. The palace servants came running to hear of our adventures; seated round the fire with a mug of tea Chhimi gave a wildly embellished account of our exploits, that held the assembled company in awestruck silence. We bathed in glory.

Fording the Bumthang River

## CHAPTER 16

The day of the long awaited birthday party for Adam and Judith had arrived. We had decided to celebrate it when I returned from Monlakarchhung as we intended to leave Bumthang within two or three days.

At 2 a.m. Adam awoke and Judith followed soon after; both were at fever pitch of excitement, demanding to be dressed to go downstairs for their birthday cake. I was still very tired from the previous day's exertions and gave them both short shrift for their disturbance, so they went to sleep again. The morning dawned beautiful and the children opened their presents in the bedroom with the sun streaming through the windows.

Sarah had bought some little dolls for Judith in Kalimpong and some roughly made pieces of dolls' furniture, which had been carefully packed away in one of the food boxes. Although composed and ladylike for her two years she was slow in her talking and understood as much Nepali, in which she conversed exclusively with Lakpa, as she did English. Her wants were few and she was a contented child, so these little presents thrilled her. She busily bathed the dolls till the cheap paint flaked off and the hair fell out; she put them to bed and dressed them so often that the poor things began to wilt.

Leppo made a beautiful boy-size bow and arrows for Adam,

carefully leaving off the metal points as we expected that, in moments of explosive anger, his sister would become a likely target. He let fly out of the window at Dolay, who sped around the garden collecting up arrows to both children's intense amusement. We had brought some wooden construction pieces from home and had acquired some small carpentry tools in an Indian bazaar. They were both amused with a cheap plastic viewer, that revolved showing tawdry pictures of Indian film stars when held against the light.

The previous evening Hochen La suggested to me that an archery match was the natural way for everyone to celebrate this red-letter day. I agreed gladly and came to realise that the only way the men could get the day off was by my invitation, as they were performing the duty of entertaining a visitor of the palace. While we were eating breakfast we saw Owya creeping along the garden wall obviously hoping to reach his den without being seen by Hochen La, who was delivering eggs to us. He had been granted two days' leave to go to his village, a day's walk away, to compete in the annual archery festival. He was now returning after six days of dawn-to-dusk shooting from which he emerged the champion. Hochen La spotted him and angrily began to upbraid him but Owya, with the smile and courtesy of the gentleman he was, produced a bottle of rakshi from the folds of his boku and he and Hochen La repaired to his den to make friends again.

Adam tried to teach Dolay how to make a car out of his construction kit, but as Dolay had never seen a car and spoke no English the problem of explanation was acute. They laughed a lot, despaired of the attempt and resorted to throwing Aloysius Bear up into a tree until he lodged in the branches; Dolay then climbed the tree with the agility of a monkey to rescue the poor bear, encouraged by the delighted yells of Adam and Judith.

Soon the men began to congregate at Drungso Chholing and we all moved over to the archery ground. I had been practising, having now played in three matches, so I felt more confident of my arrows arriving in the vicinity of the target ramp. The standard of shooting was high. Hochen La was a master; standing erect and opening his powerful shoulders with a wide draw, his arrows sped towards the target with regular accuracy scoring six hits in the day. Owya, true to his name, showed cunning and experience but less style; he stood with his feet planted widely, not close together as most men shoot; his draw was slow and deliberate with his left forefinger outstretched, guarding the arrow head on to the bow, the veins on the back of his sinewy hands standing out and his face drawn in concentration. Leppo and Dolay had the relaxed attitudes of true athletes, each shot being carried out with graceful rhythm. Rinzin was youthful and impetuous, his face contorted, his pull swift and sharp.

Regardless of their different styles the arrows cleft the air with the same soft whistle and landed with a thud round the target. Yells of joy, encouragement and despair filled the air, and once when I hit the target their show of excitement and pleasure made me feel immensely proud. At midday when the wind arose shooting became more difficult and I retired from the match to help prepare for the children's party.

Sarah had baked a birthday cake in a makeshift oven by placing three stones in the bottom of a large water pan. On these she stood a small dekchi, a round aluminium cooking pot that stacks one inside another, and placed the large pan over the embers of the fire. Using four teaspoons of baking soda the cake rose to a soft sponge of admirable lightness; powdered drinking chocolate, butter and sugar made the icing. In Kalimpong Sarah had bought some small candles for lighting in front of altars in Hindu puja; these she mounted in acorn cups we collected from Himalayan oaks; painted fir cones made a pleasant decoration round the edge of the icing. We placed six candles on the cake, four for Adam and two for Judith. The feast was supplemented with porridge biscuits, flat roti with large dollops of covetously hoarded strawberry jam and some brightly coloured jellies.

Sarah had thought of everything to make a conventional English birthday tea party in a very unconventional setting. Everything was laid out in Drungso Chholing, which we had decorated with paper chains made from porridge and jam tin labels. Adam and I spent some time putting together a cut-out frieze of Cinderella, that helped to pass the time and sub-limate his excitement. At three o'clock when the party was due to start, the princess and her younger brother arrived escorted by their bodyguard. She was a dear little girl a year older than Adam, with straight dark hair, wearing an incongruous green cardigan over her chuba. Judith and the little prince were the same age. Soon after, Dasho Thrimpon's children arrived, very shy at first but gradually warming to the noise and gaiety of the party. The candles were relit on several occasions to allow each child a turn at blowing them out, causing much amusement. An hour later the three Indian schoolmasters arrived and sat in a corner silent and unforthcoming. Finally, the archers came in and made the party go with a swing. Twenty people were crowded into our tiny hut and outside stood more who could not find room. Soon every crumb had been eaten, the teapot squeezed dry and a very happy and memorable birthday party drew to a close. The children went home, the schoolmasters took their leave and the archers stayed to play with Adam's toy cars and to build models, while Sarah and I played snakes and ladders with Ashi and Dasho Thrimpon.

Our six weeks stay in Bumthang was drawing to a close and we still had a long way to go. We were sad to say farewell to the palace servants, who had become our friends. Birka Bahadur came over from Tongsa in response to a letter I wrote asking him to take the second batch of blood to India, as he had done such a fine job transporting the first batch. This time I had packed more than three hundred specimens in six tins. We arranged for a special coolie to go with him and he would carry through exactly the same routine as he had observed the time before.

Our coolies arrived early in the morning but only two ponies could be found. Our baggage had been reduced to two-thirds the amount we had when we set out from Thimphu by steady whittling away at the stores. Chhimi went up to the dzong to see what he could arrange, while we walked round to Ashi's house, not yet completed, to say goodbye and take some photos of the children. Ashi volunteered to lend us two of her mules for the first day, to overcome the immediate problem of transport in the hope that we could find an extra pony next day. As we had to ford the river, the bridge being under repair, we assembled on the banks of the Chamkhar Chhu beside Wangdu Chholing. Two members of Ashi's bodyguard, wearing pistols at their belts, carried picnic hampers from which Thermos flasks were produced. Tea was served in delicate floral china cups off a round tray and we stood genteelly sipping it under Ashi's green parasol – a style that would have met with the approval of the Victorian travellers.

A groom led two of Ashi's mules, caparisoned with Tibetan saddle rugs, to the water's edge. These mules originally came from China to Tibet and were bought into Bhutan at great expense. Our porters and the two ponies waded into the river and found great difficulty in the strong current. Lakpa's mount lost its footing in the middle and stumbled, nearly dislodging poor Lakpa, who was very frightened. The coolies were most unhappy about the river, which reached up to their waists and was bitterly cold. Their leader, a splendidly strong and handsome six foot tall man, made sixteen crossings in order to ferry the loads of his fellows who were too afraid to return. Chhimi was most concerned at the harm the freezing water might have done to his "important thing" and vowed that he would not stir his eggs until he was sure his potency was restored.

We mounted the mules, having said goodbye to all our friends assembled on the bank to see us off and we rode into the river flowing in spate. Ashi's horseman took off his shoes, put Adam on his back and strode into the water, using my bow to steady himself against the strong current; Adam was quite amused but it looked extremely perilous half way across. Our powerful mules made little trouble of the crossing. On the far bank we reorganised ourselves and waved a final exchange to our well-wishers. This right royal send-off made a wonderful closing to our stay in Bumthang.

This was the first time I had ridden and I found it pleasant on such a strong animal. I carried Adam with me in the evening when it began to get dark and we reached the school at Gema-shong later that night.

The following morning was dull and overcast; we sadly sent Ashi's mules back with the groom. We acquired an extra mule, making our number three, all much stronger than the ponies we had hired previously. Also the porters and horsemen, who came from the village of Takhung where I had done a clinic on the Tang Chhu tour, were a stouter lot of men than ever before. Throughout the day we climbed steadily up a long ridge through rhododendron and pine forest; by mid-afternoon we reached Phope (12,600 feet), the last water and camping place before the Rudung La. The King had passed this way six years earlier and we pitched our tent on the place flattened for his camp. We were told that he travelled with about one hundred retainers and more than that number of pack animals. We baked roti bread, now Lakpa's nightly routine, ate potatoes and rice with soup from a packet and went to bed at 7 p.m. Two hours later rain began to fall so I put the flysheet over the tent and crawled in with Sarah, Lakpa and the children.

I had some apprehensions for the next day when we were to cross the Rudung La, by repute the highest and most difficult of the main passes in Bhutan. Paro Penlop told us it was not possible for "an ordinary person" to cross the pass; I was sure we belonged to this category but we now had no alternative route. Walking through fine drizzle and low cloud was disappointing as the views from the top of the pass are said to encompass the whole of the eastern mountains of Bhutan. Our wide path traversed through dank woods for an hour and then climbed more steeply up a hillside covered with rhododendron to reach the top of the pass at 13,500 feet. We found no difficulty until some yards over the far side when our troubles began.

We started a remarkable descent, skirting the bases of a number of large rocky pinnacles which stood free from the mountainside where the path was carved. Cloud swirled round the amphitheatre below us forming turbulent eddies into which the precipice where we were poised plunged; we could not see the bottom so the feeling of gaunt isolation was increased. Snow was gusting and impetuous high winds blew round us; we put the children into their anoraks, gloves and balaclavas, and prepared for the storm that was nearly upon us. Chhimi carried Judith on his back in a sling made from his dzong scarf and I put Adam in my large rucksack. The path narrowed and was cut as steps from the rock; when it took to sheer cliff a bridge was

164

Monk telling his beads
Woodman at work

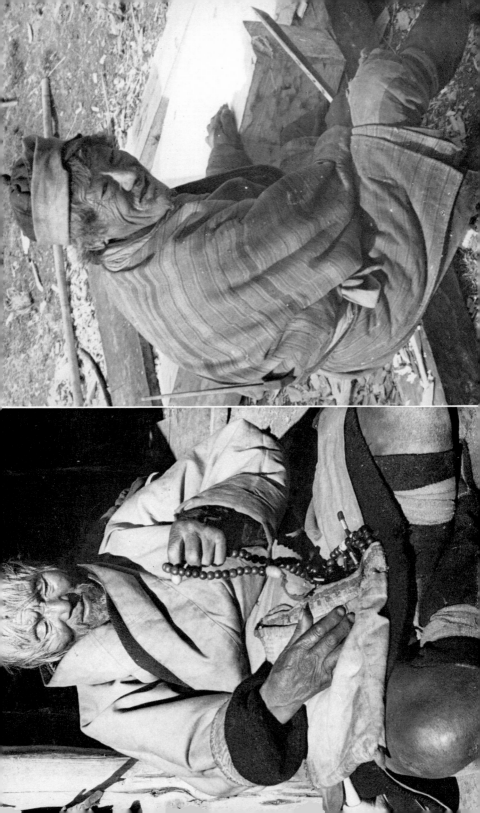

made of two logs supported away from the rockface in a delicate fashion that gave little confidence. The logs were wet and slippery, being partly snow covered; there was no hand rail for support and crossing the logs caused us alarm and Lakpa much consternation. Where the steps were obscured by snow we persuaded Lakpa and Sarah to slide down on their backsides, while Chhimi and I had to pick our way more carefully so as not to overbalance with the children. For an hour we traversed this extraordinary place that made our descent of the Tongsa steps appear like a Sunday school outing by comparison.

The dangerous part of the road gave way to wide stone steps with little exposure; after dropping a thousand feet rain took the place of snow. We stopped on a spur to eat biscuits and cold boiled potatoes and to drink tea from our Thermos – an elixir to our cold, wet and flagging spirits. Far above us, winding their way down the cliffs, we could see and hear the ponies, who were making heavy going on the difficult sections round the isolated pinnacles; below cloud boiled up out of the deep and thickly forested valley. One hour later we reached two houses on a small open meadow astride the ridge, called Pimi (10,150 feet). We were tired and damp so we cooked an enormous lunch and dried out our clothes. The house was full of porters, who had decided to shelter rather than risk the Rudung La in a storm, and the atmosphere was convivial though crowded. Some of our porters had gone on but we decided to stay although it was only noon, because clouds were gathering again for the afternoon tempest. We had Sarah's and Lakpa's bedding rolls on Adam's pony, some children's clothes in a suitcase and the two kitchen baskets.

A short while later a vicious storm broke with hail, snow, loud claps of thunder and flashes of lightning. Judith became very upset and moaned quietly in Sarah's arms as she had always been frightened by thunderstorms. Adam knelt at the window watching hailstones bouncing off the rocks and staring at the flashes that rent the melancholy sky creating a momentary brilliance. We were thankful for the shelter and thought with horror of the Rudung La under these conditions and of our porters who were probably hiding in the woods below us, there

Lhuntsi Dzong

being no houses for at least four hours. We slept and read to the children while the storm rumbled its course. By evening it was over; new snow plastered the surrounding hillsides and the Rudung La was transformed from a green hill into a spectacular white mountain. Calm followed in the wake of the wind; shafts of sunlight broke through the bases of ugly, menacing clouds, which blew away to the south making contrasting shadows on the deep timbered valleys several thousand feet below us. The somnolent grunts of the coolies and the croaking of the old hag who ran the establishment punctuated the silent peace of the night.

At 4.30 a.m. the sky was full of stars before the sun rose; I regretted the more bitterly the expansive views these conditions would have given us from the Rudung La. I was tempted to return there with my camera but decided against it and we started to descend through dense jungle to the Yungar Valley. The next four hours were perhaps the most beautiful walking of all our journey in Bhutan. The path was too steep and muddy to ride so Chhimi carried Judith much of the way; I held Adam's hand, placing him on my shoulders only in difficult places.

We passed various levels of vegetation in the 4,000 feet descent; growing in damp shaded places were many kinds of orchid hanging like creeper from the trees; rhododendrons of delicate shades and magnolias flowering in profusion coloured the woods; fragrant scents rose from this fantastic forest after the rain. Warm sunshine bathed us and, like balm, erased our miserable feelings of the previous day. By the time we reached the valley floor the heat was almost oppressive; we halted for lunch beside a rushing stream where the children took all their clothes off and splashed in a pool of clear water. Everyone seized the chance to wash themselves and their clothing.

We rose steadily in the afternoon to Chimmihlakhang, where we stayed in a small house beside a gompa overlooking the Kur Chhu. Adam was so tired I had to run beside him for the last hour to prop him up and prevent his head from flopping from side to side. Judith as usual slept, her dummy clasped firmly between her teeth, making contented sucking noises.

Our road led due north towards Lhuntsi and the weather

during the following days was unremittingly foul. Cloudless mornings beginning with promise gave way to grey skies that turned into the afternoon deluge. With no completely rainproof clothing, we had a problem to keep Sarah and the children dry and warm; Sarah's Afghan sheepskin coat shielded Judith but was sodden towards evening and became stiff and hard on drying out; I covered Adam with a leather jacket I had bought in Darjeeling, which, when zipped to his neck, made a kind of tent where he crouched, happily singing to himself or holding animated discussions with me. We had many topics for debate; the tree house we would build at my brother's farm when we returned, the condition of his muscles and how they came to be where they were, and fantastic lists of toys he wanted for his next birthday. I found some difficulty running beside him up flights of stone steps and maintaining a satisfactory dialogue.

The cave at Menchibi offered a palatial haven and refuge from the unceasing downpour of rain. A vast boulder that must have been left behind by receding glaciers of a bygone age, provided a shelter large enough to make three rooms with one open side facing the valley. Streams of water poured down the path and drips fell from the roof forming a long puddle across the mouth of the cave. All our spare clothes were wrapped in large plastic bags so we were all able to make a complete dry change. The porters built a bonfire in the centre of the cave and helped us to dry out our sodden garments and mattresses. We felt warm and secure; that delicious feeling of a winter's afternoon when you are snug indoors and can see the rain drumming on the panes of glass and the street outside glistening and running with water.

At the end of the next day the path rounded yet another corner, revealing Lhuntsi Dzong below us perched on a projecting bluff commanding access to north and south. The position was as impressive as it was oppressive, a declivity of gigantic proportions enclosed on every side by high hills. Chhimi called Lhuntsi "a corner place", aptly describing our feelings towards it during our brief stay.

Mani Wall

## CHAPTER 17

Bad news came out of Lhuntsi. The storms of the past few days that made travelling so miserable for us, played havoc with communications in Kurte district where Lhuntsi stands. The Rudung La, over which we had come, was closed. The Dong La, our intended route to Tashi Yangtsi, was impassable as we heard from some malaria-eradication officers who had just forced a way through snow four to five feet deep, passing several mules frozen dead in their tracks. The southern route down the Kur Chhu to Mongar was blocked by landslides, which had slipped two days before, cutting the main exit from the valley. So the conditions were not in our favour.

We were short of food. At Byakar we were assured that food would be available from the dzong stores but on arrival we found they had no rice, no flour, no sugar. Our own supplies had fallen to a low level as we were expecting to replenish everything from Lhuntsi Dzong for our final stage. Dasho Ramjan was in charge in the absence of the thrimpon and the nyerchen, who were in Paro attending the National Assembly; a large and genial man, he was kind and sympathetic but could not supply us with stores he did not possess. We returned to the police barracks where we were quartered and laid out all our food to estimate our daily needs. Enough remained to reach Mongar in a week if we left immediately; but this too posed problems.

First, smallpox had broken out in several of the villages further down the Kur Chhu where we must pass on our way to Mongar; the headmen forbade all travel movements through the villages in an attempt to contain the spread of the disease. We were likely to find our way barred even if we reached these villages, which lay beyond the landslides.

Second, it was reported that all local transport had been requisitioned several days before to fetch government supplies for the dzong and no animals were available in the vicinity. The food shortage was due to a famine the previous year, caused by a scourge of rats and field mice that had overrun the valley, destroyed the standing crops and eaten all the grain stores. By an edict from Thimphu, pest control officers were not allowed to use pesticides because of the Buddhist belief in the sanctity of life.

We were not a happy family party that night. We sat and discussed every aspect of our problem, reaching only one conclusion – at all costs we must leave Lhuntsi without delay. Next day Chhimi went to scour the hillsides for animals, Lakpa and Sarah searched for food, while I went to the leprosy hospital, as I had promised to do while in Thimphu.

The hospital lay an hour and a half's walk away; I collected the compounder in charge from his house on a hill above the dzong and we walked the rough road together. He talked at great speed in Nepali so I could not catch all he said, but he appeared completely dedicated to this heart-rending job he had held for eleven years. He often spoke about "creepers" and I could not understand what he was referring to. The leprosarium consisted of a small dispensary house surrounded by thirty to forty small bamboo shacks with matted roofs, scattered at random on the barren, rockstrewn mountainside; these housed the hundred and eighty patients. Not a single patch of ground was level for cultivation and the soil was so poor that nothing grew except banana trees and some very small potato plants. A trickle of water ran into a hollowed-out tree trunk providing the only source of drinking water for the camp. Inside the dispensary I was shown rows of empty tins and bottles, no medicines having arrived for several months; the few drugs that were left could only last a week or two longer. Torn strips of bandages had been washed between dressings and hung drying from a string line in one corner.

Patients slowly began to gather for a clinic and only then did the meaning of the word "creepers" dawn on me; it referred to the fifty people whose hands and feet were so mutilated by the disease that they could only shuffle about on their knees. Leprosy attacks the nerves, so fingers and toes lose feeling, become injured and eventually rot and fall off; large, indolent ulcers develop on the limbs; faces become scarred and puckered, giving the characteristic lion-like appearance; eyelids become paralysed, no longer able to blink, ulcers develop on the cornea and blindness ensues. I saw a panorama of human misery that can barely be imagined by those who have not seen it. Side by side in these overcrowded hovels were crippled grandparents with healthy children destined to become infected by the prolonged contact that is the means of spread of this insidious and horrible disease. A young mother nursing her fourth child just a few months old had nothing but the stumps of her hands, no fingers remaining. No government money had been sent to buy stores and the patient's diet had consisted of green bananas and potatoes for several months.

I wrote in my diary that day: ". . . what an assemblage of human suffering, what incalculable sadness, what a hopeless, living death." My heart bled for this devoted compounder battling out his impossible task.

I did a clinic as best I could and left behind the few medicines I had brought with me; then we visited the houses of those who were too ill to creep to the dispensary. As I was about to leave one of the patients collected an egg from every person present and handed them to me in a bowl. I had difficulty restraining the tears that welled into my eyes at that moment and to speak past the lump in my throat. I thanked them, explained that I wished no offence but could not accept the eggs and implored the patients to give them to their own children. We turned and climbed the hill and I have rarely been more sunk in gloom.

News was better on my return to Lhuntsi. Chhimi had climbed to a village an hour above the dzong and found a man who promised he could provide three mules for the following day. Lakpa and Judith had made one of their expeditions off into the country, their daily routine when we were halted, and had collected a large bundle of succulent young bracken shoots still curled in bud. Lakpa split them down the middle and cooked them in butter; they made an excellent meal, being our first green vegetable for a week. From then on we collected bracken shoots at every opportunity and these became a regular supplement to our diet.

Our evening was cheered by the visit of a prisoner from the dzong. His legs were in fetters in a manner that we had seen before: one heavy bar was fixed to two circular rings round his ankles; to ease the fifteen pounds' weight of the metal and prevent chafing a string hanging from his belt was attached to the bar, which he held in his hand, and he walked with a drunken, rolling gait accompanied by a sinister clanking noise. This man had once been a cook in the service of the King, from whom on several occasions he had stolen. When first put in the dzong he had started a business by stealing dzong stores and selling them to the public. For this supreme insult he was committed to the dzong for life and was made to wear round his neck a circular wooden board two feet in diameter, two inches thick and weighing twenty pounds. It could not be removed so the prisoner was unable to lie down to sleep, except with a very high wooden block as a pillow, and he could only feed himself with a long spoon as his hand would not reach his mouth. This amusing rascal had plaited a crown of fern leaves that made him look like a Shakespearian buffoon; having already spent fifteen years in the dzong his mind was becoming addled by his privations. On reflection this form of punishment seems just as humane as locking a man behind high walls and making him sew mailbags under the surveillance of closed circuit television for a large part of his life. By day when he was not doing work for the dzong our friend was free to roam the village and ask for food and was only locked into the dungeon at night.

In Bhutan punishment is heavy but the absence of crime and dishonesty is remarkable. Nothing was stolen from us on our entire journey nor did we ever meet a Bhutanese beggar. Severe crimes are dealt with severely but no capital punishment exists. We heard stories of murderers in the old days who used to have their right hand cut off and their heel tendons severed so that they could not run away; several years before in the Sahara I had seen an Arab who had suffered this punishment and could only shuffle about.

By contrast, punishment for simple crimes often appeared unduly harsh. A young boy called Tsewang was sent to us from the dzong as a kitchen boy; his village had disputed about grazing rights with a neighbouring village near Ura, south from here. Tsewang's village turned out to be in the wrong so one man was ordered to be sent to the dzong to be detained "on the thrimpon's pleasure". This delightful boy, who was only fourteen, had been imprisoned as a criminal in the dzong for two months already and did not know how much longer he would have to stay.

In the clear morning air, golden with the rising sun, Lhuntsi Dzong made a superb picture set against a backcloth of twenty-thousand-foot mountains to the north. The ponies arrived on time, Dasho Ramjan came to see us off and the prisoner directed operations from the pulpit-like rock. Our new head ponyman showed more authority and leadership than any before and our departure was hastened accordingly. As the path was so steep we walked down to the bridge across the Kur Chhu passing many deep purple irises growing from the banks under laurel bushes. A bamboo bridge spanned the river, which was a hundred feet wide at this point, and very deep.

Legend has it that the Kur Chhu was the eldest of three brothers, the Chamkhar Chhu being the middle brother and the Mangde or Tongsa Chhu the youngest. The three of them rested beside a big mountain in the north and before they went to sleep they decided they would next day go south to where the rice grew. The Kur Chhu left while the others were asleep, making no noise; the Chamkhar Chhu awoke and followed quickly and less

172

quietly; finally, the Mangde Chhu awoke to find the other two had left while he slept, gaining a start on him. He followed at speed with great noise; although he was the smallest of the three yet he arrived first.

We unloaded the ponies and led them across the bridge singly as it swayed several feet at the centre. Adam thought this a great joke and insisted on going back for a second crossing, though Judith was a little alarmed. Bamboo bridges are remade every three years by government order; wooden bridges are rebuilt every five years. All were in much better repair than the bridges we encountered in Nepal.

On the other side while riding past the long prayer, or mani wall, that stands beside every bridge, Lakpa's mule shied and tossed her on to a grass bank, causing her more surprise than damage. Lakpa was no horsewoman and was growing fat for lack of exercise, but we reckoned her horse worth every paise, though the men thought us mad that the ayah should ride while the sahib walked. We realised that the Sherpani who humps loads over mountain passes is never found embodied in the same person as the gentle, clean, domesticated Darjeeling girl that Lakpa was. She took the brave step of leaving home and her little boy of whom she was deeply fond, and had become a wonderful older sister to our children with whom her patience and care were inexhaustible. Never moody and growing stronger in personality as the journey proceeded, we intended to keep her in a contented frame of mind. She deserved, and won, the love and admiration of the family and she had Chhimi firmly under her thumb.

We were now equipped with three strong mules and four pack ponies, by far the best caravan we had yet acquired. Their leader was a distinguished looking man, tall and strong featured, bearing an air of authority and purpose. He wore a wide-brimmed hat with the strap hanging loosely behind his neck, his boku was a washed out mauve colour and he wore a pair of long purple stockings fading at the ankles. His appearance was so like an eminent clerical friend of mine that we called him "the Bishop" – a name he became universally known by. His colleagues were of lesser calibre but under his leadership they performed their duties adequately. One elderly Mongolian-looking gentleman with a

173

floppy peak cap usually led the line; provided he walked ahead of the pony leading it on a rein all was well, but when he dropped back and prodded it from the rear the beast objected violently and refused to budge. The third ponyman was a funny little fellow with an inane grin, who wore a jaunty trilby hat. He danced about in front of Sarah's mule, making it very excited, so early on we banished him to the middle of the line with the pack ponies and entrusted the mules to "the Bishop" and Chhimi.

Two porters carried the kitchen baskets with strict orders to remain close beside us so that whenever we stopped we could brew up tea regardless of our distance from the ponies. The men were kind to the animals, a fact that was reflected in their excellent condition. The botanist Bailey said his ponymen were "constantly talking to the animals with gentle words of encouragement"; ours certainly maintained continuous altercation with strange noises and words, but Chhimi's translation of the profanities they uttered would fall horribly on a sensitive ear. Whenever they came to a mani wall their tone changed to prayer and Adam followed their example; I once found him spinning the head of his hammer on the shaft of a screwdriver like a prayer wheel, while chanting the sacred intonations as we passed a mani wall.

Not far below the bamboo bridge we reached a bridge made of five big logs spanning the Koma Chhu where it joined the Kur Chhu. From the start Sarah's mule had shown signs of friskiness, but as it reached the bridge it threw a tantrum, prancing and bucking like a mad thing, presumably because it was frightened by the frothing white water of the small river. Judith in her usual fashion was firmly secured by her woollen christening blanket tied round her middle and knotted behind Sarah's back. The mule's hooves drummed on the logs of the bridge in startled anger; Sarah managed to slip Judith out of her blanket and threw her bodily into the arms of Chhimi, who was standing beside her trying to quieten the animal. She then slid to the ground herself and walked across the bridge, appearing calm in the face of an alarming incident. With much firm and skilful handling the ponies settled down by lunchtime with only a few minor outbursts of temper, which Sarah rode out with confidence. The cause of the trouble was a white pack pony friend of Sarah's mule that had been placed up in front; as soon as the order was re-arranged so the two friends were together we had no further trouble and peace ensued.

We followed close to the river for a while, lunched in an open meadow and continued in the afternoon climbing steeply to a cave at Chusa where we stayed the night. Several people appeared for medicines, bringing us presents of eggs in gratitude. The women gave us a pathetic assurance that they were not poisoned, a strange phenomenon we encountered on several former occasions. It appeared that certain families are branded as poisoned, the defect being inherited and passed on by females, males being exempt as with so many things in Bhutanese life. The origin seemed to be that an act of murder or similar crime had occurred in the family several generations before. If you receive food from a person with a poisoned palm the food is likely to harm you, so Chhimi was always most careful to find out about the giver. This tragic form of superstition, particularly prevalent in the Kurte district where we were, makes complete social outlaws of many pleasant and innocent people. That night, for the first time on our journey, I felt ill with fever and stomach cramps and the men were convinced I had been poisoned. I curled up in a corner of the cave and wished for nothing but to be left alone, envisaging, as doctors will, the multitude of fearful diseases from which I might be suffering.

One of the pack ponies was also ill; he had been going badly all day and I saw the ponyman make a large cut in the animal's ear from which blood flowed, supposedly letting out the evil humours causing the animal's sickness. He also lit a fire of dried leaves and held it under the pony's nose, making him inhale the acrid smoke. Despite these measures the poor beast was still too ill to accompany us next day so we left him behind. I was much better in the morning and had completely thrown off my lethargy. Sarah suffered from a painful, swollen foot, due to an infected insect bite that caused her difficulty in putting on her long leather boots.

The path rose and fell next day keeping close to the river until Paktsan, from where a four-hour climb brought us to Wambur

(6,420 feet) by late afternoon. For the first time in several days only light rain fell and there seemed a real chance that the weather would improve so that we would see the view in the morning. We camped on the crest of a hill beside a small chorten looking many miles up the stupendous valley on the Kur Chhu; our path was now turning away from sight of the mountains so we wanted to give ourselves one last chance. The ponymen erected a shelter from bamboo because they were reluctant to go down to the village close at hand that was rumoured to be infected with smallpox. High above the valley, illumined by occasional shafts of moonlight breaking through the clouds, Sarah and I played chess by the light of the fire.

A downpour started; by 3 a.m. my sleeping bag was sodden as I was on the windward side of the shelter, protected only by a pile of pony saddles. I crawled into the tent to wait for the dawn, which came reluctantly through sheeting rain. A huddle of disconsolate ponymen sat round a small fire trying to keep the smoke out of their eyes and gain a little warmth before tackling the tedious business of saddling up. We ate some damp and tasteless roti, which had been cooked the night before and left out in the rain, to assuage our hunger until we would reach Domkar school where we could dry out and cook a meal.

After a while we met a man and two ponies at a narrow place in the path, coming in the opposite direction. On hearing where we were going he began to gesticulate wildly with excited grimaces and a tone of horror. We realised all was not well with the coming road. Chhimi eventually translated his conversation, from which we discovered that a large part of the road ahead had been washed out by landslides and we would have to portage our loads for much of the next day past Owtsho. The prospect was not encouraging but as the only alternatives were a retreat to Lhuntsi, the snowbound Rudung La or Dong La, or north to Tibet, it seemed better to press on. The rain had started again and the expedition took on the gloomy appearance of a desperate escape from an enclosed valley with few exits.

At Domkar school the masters kindly lent us their kitchen to cook in and dry out our clothes. Many of the children were away from school because of the shortage of food; normally they stay in huts behind the school and their families provide them with rations and firewood during term-time, but now very few parents could spare the necessary food.

From Domkar the road plummeted 1,500 feet to the river by a series of zig-zag bends. We left Chhimi and "the Bishop" to negotiate with the village headman for porters to help us over the landslides next day. A pleasant path led through woods until we began to enter the gorge where the Kur Chhu plunged into a narrow ravine confined by perpendicular rock walls. Our path was cut out of the cliff face for a quarter of a mile, hanging two hundred feet vertically above the torrent. A six-inch wall guarded the outside edge and the roof was frequently so low we had to stoop to pass. I tied a dzong scarf round Adam's middle in case he should trip and pull his hand out of mine, for the river would have offered no comfort as a landing-place, and we walked slowly across. Having passed the exposed place, where Lakpa became very frightened, we dropped to the river and soon reached Owtsho, a large open meadow encircled with pine trees. We shared a cowherd's shelter built on stilts beside a chorten with a grumpy old man who appeared to resent our intrusion. He turned out to be the headman of the village that was obliged to provide porters for the next day, but he made no attempt to co-operate with our requests; "the Bishop" and Chhimi delivered a forceful harangue but the obtuse fellow would offer no promises of help.

We made a pot of tea, that tasted foully of washing soap. I felt apprehensive of the morrow. Everyone was thinking of the landslides ahead and the atmosphere was tense.

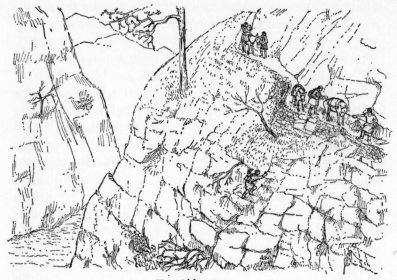

Kur Chhu Gorge

# CHAPTER 18

In the early hours of the morning as I tried to open an eye to survey the prospects for the day, I felt as I had done on many occasions before Alpine climbs. The fear of the unknown, enhanced by reports of men just returned with stories of the horrors they had experienced, would increase my own fear and weaken my resolve so that all I wanted to do was to bury my head under the pillow again and pray that the weather would be too bad to leave the warmth and safety of the hut. Circumstances were different now and delay could solve none of our problems; the quicker we grappled with the gorge the better.

We left Owtsho at 6.30 a.m. under threatening, cloud-laden skies; half an hour later the rain started. Only one coolie turned up instead of the promised ten – not a good start to the day. The first obstruction was a large pine tree that had fallen across the path on a steep grassy section of hillside; the gap was too low for the ponies to pass under and the banks too high for them to climb round while laden. So we sheltered Sarah and the children under the fallen tree-trunk and unloaded every pony, leading them up the slippery bank and round to the path on the other side. Each loading and unloading took a full half hour of heavy work.

Chhimi and I went ahead to reconnoitre the path and less than half a mile distant we encountered the first landslide. A stream bed had been converted into a torrent by the prodigious rainfall and had carried an avalanche of rocks and mud across the path, leaving only a deep and dirty scar where the road had been. The place was well set back from the cliff edge with no unpleasant exposure, although the ground was steep and loose. I slid down a muddy bank into the stream bed twenty feet below the path, picked a way between large boulders and clambered up the wet, grassy slope opposite by pulling on grass and bamboo roots. A few yards beyond the slip I found a large rock beside the path offering a dry lee side and a small fox hole. We brought the family across and settled them under the overhanging roof of rock out of the pouring rain; Adam crawled into the hole where he could just lie full length, and made himself comfortable. The horses slithered into the watercourse but they found the further grassy bank difficult, so we positioned the men at strategic points where they could pull or shove the animals as they grappled for a foothold.

From the description of the man we had met the previous day we estimated the most serious landslide was about a mile further on; Chhimi went ahead and later returned with a woeful look on his face; "the Bishop" and I followed him to devise a plan of campaign. Rounding a corner our path came to an abrupt end at a place where the cliff fell precipitously three to four hundred feet into the raging Kur Chhu; a huge section of the hillside had slipped, carrying everything before it; between us and the intact path a hundred yards beyond was a tangled mass of boulders, tree trunks and mud poised insecurely on the sloping mountainside.

I noticed a cave above the path so I climbed up to see if it would make a suitable refuge for the family, as I estimated crossing this landslide would take us several hours; it was small but dry and I gathered enough kindling sticks to start a fire. Chhimi and I returned to lead Sarah, Lakpa and the children up the slippery and holdless grass; they felt cold because of their enforced inactivity having to wait under the cramped rock and because of the dampness of the air. The rain was beginning to relent and a thin column of smoke rose from the mouth of the cave above us indicating some warmth and comfort ahead. Leaving the children in Lakpa's care, Sarah came down to help with the animals that had been unloaded and were nervously stamping the ground, sensitive of something strange afoot.

The first mule started off with "the Bishop" leading it by the halter and Chhimi hanging on to its tail. For twenty feet the mule balanced on a thin rocky ledge, which broke into steps having once been the upward bank of the path. "The Bishop" reassured and coaxed the animal while Chhimi held its tail firmly in case of a slip, because at this particular point nothing could prevent an unbroken plunge down the cliffside into the river. Rock gave place to a thirty foot bank of earth and battered debris into which I had cut steps with the ice axe, but the soil was not secure enough to hold for many passages. The mule performed an ungainly glissade on all fours with Chhimi still hanging on to its tail and following at speed to the bottom of the old watercourse where it was comparatively safe; the stream bed was filled with boulders, some as big as a house, round which we passed to the further bank. We then shoved and pulled the frightened mule upwards, circumvented a projecting corner and reaching the path that had originally been carved from the rockface; now two feet wide and with the inclination sloping outwards to the cliff edge, it offered no security.

When we looked at the section we had traversed I realised that no turning back was possible and we were totally committed to reaching Mongar whatever might stand in our way. Sarah then led her mule across with the little old man at the tail end; two hours later all the animals were assembled together. I returned with the men to help carry the sixty pound loads; balancing on the slippery outward sloping mud with no hands free for support made hard work. With the assistance of the ten porters we had hoped for the whole exercise would have been immeasurably simpler and more quickly completed.

We decided to rest as the rain had eased, so we returned to our cave for some jam and roti sandwiches and a cup of tea, which still tasted of soap. The new coolie came with us to help escort the children; he was immensely strong and sure-footed and tied Adam firmly on to his back and danced across the rocks and mud with no concern for the vertiginous situation. Adam thought this whole performance a lot of fun; Judith slept on Chhimi's back.

Having gained the safety of the further path we met "the Bishop"; his face was horror-struck and he talked with great agitation, making excited gestures. A few yards on was a smaller slip where some stakes had been driven into the bank and the path remade by resting two thin saplings on the stakes; this temporary gangway was probably made by the man we met near Domkar to enable him to cross this nasty section of the landslide. Chhimi translated "the Bishop's" story: one of the ponies had slipped on the wet logs and its back legs fell over the edge; as it slewed round the outside load broke free and bounced one hundred and fifty feet down the cliff, miraculously coming to rest on a ledge eighty feet above the river where its fall was broken by a small fir tree. "The Bishop" saved the pony by grabbing its tail and hauling it bodily back on to the logs from where it scrambled to level ground. He was deeply upset so I assured him we would immediately go in search of the missing load. When we reached the place we looked over the edge and saw the little old man struggling up the broken cliff with the box on his back; he had shown no sign of initiative ever before, but this was a very brave and generous gesture. He beamed with pride and pleasure when we thanked and congratulated him on his courage.

When the trunk was recovered, a look of disgust crept over the men's faces as they saw blood seeping through the outer covering of sacking and dripping on to the ground. This box held the medicines and my blood specimens from Lhuntsi, which I reckoned must all be broken. The most important item in the trunk was the book in which I had written my goitre and blood results, and I was thankful that I had kept a carbon copy of these facts and of my diary in a separate place in case of such an event. Nothing remained to do but to laugh heartily and relieve the tension of the preceeding strained hours.

We were now past the worst landslides and only two more places remained where complete unloading was necessary. We descended to the river, found a flat place where we laid out all our clothes in the sun that had just appeared and cooked a feast of rice, potatoes and bracken shoots with some onion leaves we had saved from Lhuntsi. We opened a tin of corned beef, which in the present circumstances tasted like fillet steak. Adam and Judith ran round naked in the sun, their white bottoms contrasting with the dark tanned faces of the ponymen among whom they played.

I remembered Eric Shipton's exciting description of the Rishi Gorge he passed through on his first entry into the sanctuary of Nanda Devi, and I wondered what he would have thought of our gorge.

The three miles of path across the landslides took up eleven hours of almost continuous work. We decided to travel no further than Rewan that night where we could shelter in the leeside of a big rock; everyone was relaxed after the strains of the day and we sat round the blazing log fire singing and joking. I wrote in my diary that night:

"For the family the dangers of the gorge were considerable but not excessive, every precaution was taken to make their passage safe. Without such splendid ponymen and our indefatigable Chhimi, the problems might have been much worse. Sarah was great. Never did she complain or blame me for the situation we were in; she was calm throughout and kept the children warm and happy where many mothers would have thrown in the sponge and wept. I was as frightened as I have been on any mountain but, being up to our neck in it, we could do nothing but press on and get out of Lhuntsi quickly, the alternatives being too unpleasant to contemplate . . . Luck was against us and I have achieved little of what I hoped for. We have had an unplanned adventure from which we have escaped unscathed and perhaps in a strange way this compensates for our lack of success in mapping and medicine."

We left Rewan and climbed towards a pass that overlooked Tormashong; we particularly wanted to avoid the villages near here, which were reported to be the focus of the smallpox outbreak. Diseased persons were sent off into the woods to live in primitive shelters they had to build for themselves; food was left in the open for them to collect if they were well enough to move, if not, they died. This apparently brutal form of treatment was the only known way to curb the spread of such an infectious disease when so few people were vaccinated; many who had been driven into the woods were dying and a pathetic atmosphere of calamity prevailed in the panic-stricken region.

We saw Mongar Dzong in the distance as we rounded a hillside, leaving the Kur Chhu to sweep its way southwards. We thankfully arrived there at the end of eleven hours marching – a long day for the children, who were very tired. We stayed in the brand new guest house of the dzong, that was being built in the best tradition of Bhutanese artistry and craftsmanship. Our rest day at Mongar was passed pleasantly observing the workmen and aimlessly wandering through the village. Our immediate impression was one of order and cleanliness; the dzong was newly whitewashed, a brand new school hostel holding eighty boys stood close by, the dispensary, wireless station and school were grouped together giving an appearance of efficient organisation. The Mongar thrimpon has a reputation for being a wise and far-sighted man, a fact we appreciated when we met him in Tashigang a few days later; he had bought several hundred loads of rice on the Indian border, transported them to Tashigang by army vehicles and was arranging for ponies to carry them to his famine-stricken region.

April was now drawing to a close and the last short stage of our journey lay ahead. Half an hour after we left Mongar under grey skies the heavens opened in a torrential downpour that soaked through all clothing to our skin; we covered the children as best we could but to no avail in such a cloudburst. We followed the path through forest, thankful that we were too early in the season for leeches, which these trees would harbour prolifically at the height of the monsoon. Morale sank to a low ebb as water permeated our last layers of dry clothing and trickled down our necks. No house could be found for shelter from the storm so we sent Chhimi ahead to a village an hour further up the pass to prepare a fire and hot water.

At last blue chinks appeared in the melancholy sky and sunlight broke through the clouds, offering us a ray of hope for more clement weather ahead. We crossed the Kori La (7,900 feet) in bright sunshine and followed a way through a pretty forest arriving at Shirizampa (3,220 feet) by evening. As the clouds were again menacing and full of rain, Chhimi evicted some poor coolies from under the only available roof and established himself as guardian of the precincts on our behalf. On such occasions we blessed Chhimi's extroverted and despotic character; I was amazed that a boy of his years could hold so much authority with adult men. The cantilever bridge over the Shiri Chhu had been destroyed in the floods of the year before and now only disrupted giant timbers remained, sticking out of the piers at ungainly angles, clearly exposing details of the complicated construction as only a ruin can. A temporary bamboo swinging bridge took its place, which we crossed the following morning.

The day followed the familiar pattern of a tedious four-thousand-foot climb in the morning to the Bageng La, then a similar descent in the afternoon – something akin to climbing Ben Nevis each day and returning to sleep at Fort William, for many days on end. Although the children's highest altitude reached was modest they aggregated several Everests during the journey and, on footage alone, should be qualified to join any mountaineering club in the world.

We camped at Yayung beside the Manas or Dangme Chhu, the largest river in Bhutan, which drains the mountains of the east. As it was our last night on the road we feasted on the few goodies that remained; rice heavily laced with sweet mango chutney, roti cakes thickly spread with jam and our last tin of corned beef made into a stew with dried peas. Our delight at the prospect of seeing Tashigang next day was strangely turned to sourness when we met a jeep on the newly constructed piece of road beside the river. The ponies took fright and nearly came to grief in their attempt to flee; Adam and Judith suddenly became wildly excited; we had arrived in civilisation and were not sure we wanted to be there after all.

Prayer Flags and Chorten

## CHAPTER 19

Tashigang Dzong, spectacularly placed on a long spur a thousand feet above the Manas River, seemed a fitting goal as the climax of our journey. We climbed to the dzong and passed through the gates with the feeling of a triumphant army arriving home.

"Where have you come from?" we were asked by a man crossing the courtyard.

"From Thimphu," we replied with a casual air.

"From Thimphu! Never!" he exclaimed, looking at Sarah and the children, and ran off to tell his friends. Word soon spread; passing through the dzong we rode up the hill beyond to the guest house, people gathered to wish us well and we felt gratitude and pride. Father Mackey, the headmaster of the government school, came running down to welcome us; we were invited to a lunch prepared in our honour by the Iranian doctor's wife.

After so many weeks on our own away from news it was difficult to hold a discussion on affairs in the outside world but we rejoiced in such pleasant company. After lunch we visited the school, run for the government by Canadian Jesuit priests; Father Mackey is an extroverted character full of enthusiasm and humour to whom we warmed instantly; like so many priests in the Canadian bush he is tough, yet resilient and imaginative. He was assisted by Father Coffey and Brother Quinn, who was in the Royal Canadian Mounted Police as a young man and had travelled all over Baffin Land by dog-team and sailed up the northern coast of Labrador; we spent a happy hour reliving adventures and experiences in the barren north.

The school was run on the lines of a college in Darjeeling where the Fathers had taught before being invited by the King to come into Bhutan; the boys were learning such subjects as gymnastics, chemistry and Shakespearean drama with intense zeal and pleasure. A new high school was being built twenty miles down the road at Sherubtse whither the Fathers were to move when the school was finished.

Father Mackey's philosophy towards the religion of his boys was tolerant and enlightened compared with some of the missionary attitudes we had met before. He considered he was in Bhutan to teach and not to proselytise, as he had promised not to do. I had noticed that the verandah outside Father's room was always occupied by boys playing chess or reading his books and the door of his room was never closed, so he had no privacy even while saying Mass. He was a close friend of the omze, or abbot, of Tashigang and had made extensive studies of the local religious customs, legends and the lama's dances that are famous in Bhutan.

From schools such as this will rise Bhutan's new generation of trained professional and technical men who must guide the country into her new twentieth century role; Tashigang will doubtless contribute its share, and promises to be a model school of northern India.

We enjoyed our leisure in Tashigang, going from one party to another; birthdays and celebrations seemed to happen in a miraculous fashion and we were entertained royally.

In order to round off my goitre work I wished to visit some villages in a valley to the east, on the way towards Merak Sakteng. "The Bishop" volunteered to accompany Chhimi and me so one fine morning we set out to walk towards East Bhutan's border with India's North East Frontier Agency, where the Chinese invaded in 1962. My aim was to reach two villages reported to have an exceptionally high incidence of goitre and also to visit the homes of a nomadic, tribal people called the Brokpas.

The first day we reached Phome after eight hours walking along the beautiful and fertile valley of the Gamri Chhu. The village headman had called all the goitre patients, but as none had arrived by the following morning we asked him to gather them for our return. From Phome we entered a narrow valley and climbed steadily through new-leafed forest beside a tumbling river. Many Brokpas passed us carrying loads towards Tashigang. They are jangali looking people with strong bone features; they wear a characteristic hat made of yak hair like a thick skull cap with five woven prongs projecting sideways to drain the water away from their shoulders; a purple cloth coat belted at the waist is covered with a skin waistcoat and they have short pants with a split up the side and long leggings and boots also made from hides. The Brokpas are Bhutanese people but of Tibetan stock with individual customs and a different language; they live at high altitudes tending cattle and yak, following them nomadically between their seasonal pastures; they also carry on trade between Tawang in N.E.F.A. and East Bhutan.

At Sakteng we suddenly broke out of the deep-cut forested valley where masses of rhododendrons were in full flower, onto an open alpine meadow and a glacial valley surrounded by many snow-clad mountains. The snow was lying at 11–12,000 feet, exceptionally low for May, and this reinforced my opinion that our venture this year would be a disastrous washout if we had been purely interested in climbing.

We slept at the Bhutanese army camp at 10,200 feet where we met a friend of Chhimi's from Bumthang, so we were well entertained with rakshi and rude humour.

At 6.30 a.m. the next day we started back, immediately setting a brisk pace having been told that to reach Tashigang would take two days. Chhimi's and my unspoken thoughts were identical – Tashigang by nightfall. We raced on, reaching Phome at 12.15 p.m.; still no patients had arrived although they had been called by the headman. He explained the reason: coincident with our arrival in Tashigang, a "headhunter's scare" swept down the valley like a flood tide, paralysing the people with fear. Rumour was abroad that hunters were coming to collect heads in Bhutan to take to India to feed to the trains in order to make them go faster; the hunters were thought mainly to be Indians but any foreigner was suspect. The rumour started in Thimphu not long before, where a Bhutanese soldier going to the bazaar one night was set upon by some Nepali Drukpa labourers, who thought he was hunting for heads. Fantastic stories spread like wildfire across the country into every region; hospitals emptied overnight and nobody would go out after dark; Chhimi was so frightened to relieve himself at night that he woke up "the Bishop" to accompany him outside. As I was suspected of being a head-hunter, and a known blood-sucker to boot, no one would come near me; this might have seemed amusing but for the serious effects it had on my research work. On top of the disastrous loss of all my specimens from Lhuntsi and our inability to remain there long enough to do a goitre survey, the present situation meant that my plan for the entire east of Bhutan had been a failure. Easy though it was to appreciate the problem on the spot, I realised how difficult it would be to explain to my sponsors at home the hardluck story of our lack of results in this region.

We ate and rested for an hour at Phome, then walked fast and steadily to Radhi and reached Luntsen Zampa feeling very tired at 6 p.m. as evening was approaching. We cooked a large bowl of soup and walked on in the dark along a narrow path above the river, which we could hear roaring below. I was afraid of missing my step, tripping in the blackness and falling over the edge, especially as weariness was blunting our judgment. At last we came to the chorten from where we saw the lights of Tashigang a thousand feet above us.

The crux of our pilgrimage, which I prefer to forget, was the climb up the final hill; we reached the guest house at 8.30 p.m., exactly fourteen hours after departing from Sakteng. This was our final masochistic fling sealing a bond of friendship between Chhimi, "the Bishop" and me: I am powerless to explain its depth in words; but I had known two exceptionally fine men.

Two letters were waiting for me on my return: one was from Dr. Mourant to say the Bumthang blood specimens had not arrived; the other was from Robin Morris, the B.O.A.C. manager at Dum Dum airport, Calcutta, who had handled all my previous specimens with efficiency and speed, telling me a woeful tale. Dr. Mourant had cabled him to enquire why my last batch had not arrived; Robin Morris had investigated the matter immediately and discovered the entire consignment had been sitting for three weeks of India's hottest month under the tin roof of a warehouse of the airfreight company. Birka Bahadur had again done his part without fault; the specimens had reached a a hangar at Calcutta airport less than one hundred yards across the tarmac from the B.O.A.C. office, where on receipt Robin Morris would have sent them, refrigerated, on the next plane to London; but some bureaucratic idiot had failed to read the labels and my precious work of several months, many hundreds of miles and much toil, was jettisoned into a corner to incubate and rot. This unique collection of specimens was almost completely useless when they eventually reached London; only a fraction of the tests could be performed on them.

In that bitter moment I swallowed hard and swore vehemently to relieve my pent up feelings. But not everything was lost. Some interesting facts came out of my goitre work in the middle of Bhutan; I had treated with iodised oil a large number of patients whom I intend to follow up later and, if it proves a successful method of treatment, to recommend its widespread use in Bhutan; fascinating results have come out of the blood work though only about half my six hundred specimens were testable. As expected, I received little solace on my return. My mentors were interested in the problems we had faced but were too saddened by the loss of their precious specimens to be sympathetic. I wrote a report on my work for The Royal Society that must have appeared ridiculously melodramatic with talk of boxes of blood falling down landslides, snowbound passes, headhunters and hothouses.

But we had crossed Bhutan from west to east on our own, among the very few European travellers to do so; we had mapped the virgin peaks of Monlakarchhung; we had reached our goal with many difficulties but no disasters. We had suffered the ill-fortune to run into an early monsoon with extraordinary weather for the time of year in Bhutan, but this was a mixed blessing. If the snow had fallen early we would have found the western passes much more difficult; but the usual clear pre-monsoon weather of April and early May never appeared and one storm ran into another until the monsoon was upon us.

We had tasted liberty but we were soon to lose it. For four months we had been free of the encumbrances of the outside world; we had gone where we wanted, stopped, ate, slept where we pleased; we had been masters of our own destiny. Now we would have to be disciplined by the demands of the civilised world we were returning to. As a family we had travelled among people who regard travelling families as a natural phenomenon; we came to them not as explorers or mountaineers, and as a family they had accepted us; as a family we had shared our highest moments of exhilaration and joy, our lowest ebb of fear and disappointment.

Chhimi and Lakpa had been part of our family – I say this without being patronising – they shared every experience and without them the success of our venture would surely not have been achieved.

We left Tashigang and drove to the border, catching a second class train from Gauhati to Hashimara. Chhimi had never seen a train before and travelled in the luggage rack with Adam and me. The girls slept below and were robbed of a hundred rupees during the night. Our train ambled across the Dooars and we reached Phuntsoling to find the road to Thimphu had been washed away, so we could not give a report on our work in person to the King.

We returned to England thinking our journey had been formidable, but England seemed parochial and uninterested.

"Oh, you've just been to Bhutan. Do tell us *all* about it. Did you stay in some nice hotels? I hope your car went well on those awful roads. We've been having such dreadful weather recently . . ."

For a year we retired into silence, determined not to become travel bores – so few people truly wanted to know.

Quite suddenly I saw that I must write it all down for the children to read one wet afternoon, when those wonderful days they unknowingly contributed so much towards have long since faded from their memories and disappeared beyond their expanding horizon.